THE PHOTOGRAPHS: Here are unforgettable photographs of the face of war: a shattered, wailing Chinese woman left desolate by the bombing of Singapore, a Nazi officer barking orders despite his wounds and blood-drenched uniform, a German soldier lying frozen in the snow outside Stalingrad, the somber Roosevelt asking Congress for a declaration of war on Japan, long lines of soldiers on Corregidor being marched into captivity, and men in North Africa embracing the flat, unyielding desert for cover.

THE WORDS: This volume includes some of history's most famous phrases: Churchill's magnificent "Their finest hour," selections from FDR's "Day of infamy" and "Four freedoms" speeches, and MacArthur's immortal "I shall return." There are also an American pilot's action-packed description of his "30 seconds over Tokyo," the terrifying words of a Luftwaffe officer joyously predicting the total annihilation of London, Robert St. John on the bombing of Belgrade and Alan Moorehead's brilliant reporting of the horror of the desert war.

D0033211

Eyewitness History Of World War II

Vol. 2
Siege

BY ABRAHAM ROTHBERG
PICTURES: PIERCE G. FREDERICKS
MICHAEL O'KEEFE
DESIGN: ANTHONY LaROTONDA

BANTAM BOOKS, INC.
NEW YORK / TORONTO / LONDON

contents

EYEWITNESS HISTORY OF
WORLD WAR II / Volume 2: SIEGE

RLI: | VLM 10 (VLR 8-10) |
     | --- |
     | IL 8-adult |

Bantam edition / October 1966;
second printing July 1967; third printing September
1969; fourth printing September 1970; fifth printing
March 1971; sixth printing September 1972; seventh
printing December 1973; eighth printing July 1974;
ninth printing July 1976; tenth printing July 1977.

ISBN 0-553-11306-2

Published simultaneously in the United States
and Canada.

Bantam Books are published by Bantam Books, Inc.
Its trademark, consisting of the words "Bantam
Books" and the portrayal of a bantam, is registered
in the United States Patent Office and in other
countries. Marca Registrada. Bantam Books, Inc.,
666 Fifth Avenue, New York, New York 10019.

Printed in the United States of America.

0 9 8 7 6 5 4 3 2 1

1.
2.
3.
4.

Their Finest Hour

The Battle of Britain

With the fall of France, Britain stood alone. Only the island bastion, "that fortress built by nature against infection and the hand of war," was left to resist the Nazi legions. Although most of the British armies had been rescued at Dunkirk, its tanks, armor, and heavy equipment had been abandoned. Britain was in desperate straits. Only the Royal Navy and the Royal Air Force stood between a powerful Wehrmacht and the cliffs of Dover. Hitler was sure that Britain would now come to terms. He was counting on appeasement and the "peace party" in England to ask for a negotiated peace. He had been so certain all along that he had even neglected to make provisions for a cross-Channel invasion before France fell.

On July 19, a scant month after the French had been humiliated at Compiègne, Hitler made a speech to the Reichstag offering Great Britain peace:

In this hour I feel it to be my duty before my own conscience to appeal once more to reason and common sense in Great Britain as much as elsewhere. I consider myself in a position to make this appeal, since I am not a vanquished foe begging favors, but the victor, speaking in the name of reason. I can see no reason why this war need go on. . . .

At the same time German peace feelers were put out through Sweden, the United States, and the Vatican.

After the fall of France, Hitler tried to bomb Great Britain into submission.

Three days later Lord Halifax brushed the offer aside. No peace would be acceptable to Britain, he said, which left Nazis in control of any non-German territories. But the real reply and the key to British spirit had been made a few weeks before in Winston Churchill's burning oratory:

... The battle of France is over. I expect that the **Battle of Britain is about to begin. Upon this battle**

Chief of the Luftwaffe, Hermann Göring (sixth from the right, turned towards

depends the survival of Christian civilization. Upon it depends our British life, and the long continuity of our institutions and our Empire. The whole fury and might of the enemy must very soon be turned on us. Hitler knows that he will have to break us in this Island or lose the war. If we can stand up to him, all Europe may be free and the life of the world may move forward into broad, sunlit uplands. But if we fail, then the whole

camera) on the French coast, just twenty miles from the cliffs of Dover (rear).

world, including the United States, including all that we have known and cared for, will sink into the abyss of a new Dark Age made more sinister, and perhaps more protracted, by the lights of perverted science. Let us therefore brace ourselves to our duties, and so bear ourselves that, if the British Empire and its Commonwealth last for a thousand years, men will still say, "This was their finest hour."

Hitler already had a plan to invade the British Isles: "Operation Sea Lion." To make it effective required command of the air and sea, particularly over the area chosen as the "invasion coast," and a huge fleet to transport, convoy and land the Wehrmacht across the English Channel under the Luftwaffe umbrella, and then to protect the lines of supply. Though Nazi soldiers were singing "We're sailing for England," doing so was considerably more difficult.

Both the German Navy and the Wehrmacht insisted that mastery of the skies was the first essential. Hitler, therefore, decided to use Göring's Luftwaffe to destroy the RAF, to soften Britain up for invasion, and in the process destroy the people's morale so that the government would be forced to sue for peace. Everything — invasion or capitulation — depended on victory in the air. "Operation Sea Lion" counted on achieving air supremacy during the summer, then invading at the best time, mid-September, when the moon was full and the tides high. While the Luftwaffe was destroying the RAF, the Navy would have two months to assemble leading craft for invasion and the Wehrmacht time to train its troops in amphibious assault.

The air battle of Britain went through three stages. In the first, through July and August 1940, the Luftwaffe hammered the south coast of England, the projected invasion site, and battered ships, docks, and harbor facilities. In doing so the German air force tried to engage the RAF and deplete the Fighter Command's strength. The second phase, in August and September, was directed at the Fighter Command itself, its planes, ground organization, and airfields. The Luftwaffe tried to annihilate the RAF and sweep its fighters from the sky. When the first two phases failed, the Luftwaffe, in the last phase, turned its fury on the great cities, ports, and industrial centers.

Though the Germans had 2670 planes to their 1475, the RAF did not surrender the skies and the British people refused to be cowed. As wave on wave of Dornier, Heinkel, and Stuka bombers came, protected by swarms of Messerschmitt and Focke-Wulf fighters, the RAF's Spitfires and Hurricanes intercepted them and shot many out of the skies. For every plane the RAF lost, it shot down two German aircraft, and while the British were able to save most of their pilots, the Germans lost far more than they could afford. To those valiant RAF fliers, Winston Churchill paid glowing tribute:

The gratitude of every home in our Island, in our Empire, and indeed throughout the world, except in the abodes of the guilty, goes out to the British airmen who, undaunted by odds, unwearied in their constant challenge and mortal danger, are turning the tide of the World War by their prowess and by their devotion. Never in the field of human conflict was so much owed by so many to so few.

Balloon barrages, anti-aircraft fire and the secret development of radar by British scientists, so that enemy planes could be rapidly spotted and intercepted, all were part of an air defense in which the thin line of Spitfires and Hurricanes fought for the sky.

John Beard, a flying officer, tells about his defense

of the skies over London:

We were flying in four V formations of three. I was flying No. 3 in Red flight, which was the squadron leader's and thus the leading flight. On we went, wing tips to left and right slowly rising and falling, the roar of our twelve Merlins drowning all other sound. We crossed over London, which, at 20,000 feet, seemed just a haze of smoke from its countless chimneys, with nothing visible except the faint glint of the barrage balloons and the wriggly silver line of the Thames. . . .

Minutes went by. Green fields and roads were now beneath us. I scanned the sky and the horizon for the first glimpse of the Germans. A new vector came through on the radio telephone and we swung round with the sun behind us. Swift on the heels of this I heard Yellow flight leader call through the earphones. I looked quickly toward Yellow's position, and there they were! . . .

The squadron leader's voice came through the earphones, giving tactical orders. We swung round in a great circle to attack on their beam—into the thick of them. Then, on the order, down we went. I took my hand from the throttle lever so as to get both hands on the stick, and my thumb played neatly across the gun button. You have to steady a fighter just as you have to steady a rifle before you fire it.

I had an instant's flash of amazement at the Heinkel proceeding so regularly on its way with a fighter on its tail. "Why doesn't the fool move?" I thought, and actually caught myself flexing my muscles into the action I would have taken had I been he.

When he was square across the sight I pressed the button. There was a smooth trembling of my Hurricane as the eight-gun squirt shot out. I gave him a two-second burst and then another. Cordite fumes blew

The British were the first to use radar to detect enemy aircraft at night.

A barrage balloon, to harass low planes, rises over England's Tower Bridge.

back into the cockpit, making an acrid mixture with the smell of hot oil and the air-compressors.

I saw my first burst go in and, just as I was on top of him and turning away, I noticed a red glow inside the bomber. I turned tightly into position again and now saw several short tongues of flames lick out along the fuselage. Then he went down in a spin, blanketed with smoke and with pieces flying off.

I left him plummeting down and, horsing back on my stick, climbed up again for more. The sky was clearing, but ahead toward London I saw a small, tight formation of bombers completely encircled by a ring of Messerschmitts. They were still heading north. As I raced forward, three flights of Spitfires came zooming up from beneath them in a sort of Prince-of-Wales's-feathers maneuver. They burst through upward and outward, their guns going all the time. They must have each got one, for an instant later I saw the most extraordinary sight of eight German bombers and fighters diving earthward together in flames.

I turned away again and streaked after some distant specks ahead. Diving down, I noticed that the running progress of the battle had brought me over London again. I could see the network of streets with the green space of Kensington Gardens, and I had an instant's glimpse of the Round Pond, where I sailed boats when I was a child. In that moment, and as I was rapidly overhauling the Germans ahead, a Dornier 17 sped right across my line of flight, closely pursued by a Hurricane. And behind the Hurricane came two Messerschmitts. He was too intent to have seen them and they had not seen me! They were coming slightly toward me. It was perfect. A kick at the rudder and I swung in toward them, thumbed the gun button, and let them have it. The first burst was placed just the right distance ahead of the leading Messerschmitt. He ran slap into it and he simply came to pieces in the air. His companion, with one of the speediest and most brilliant "get-outs" I have ever seen, went right away in a half-Immelmann turn. I missed him completely. He must almost have been hit by the pieces of the leader but he got away. I hand it to him.

At that moment some instinct made me glance up at my rear-view mirror and spot two Messerschmitts closing in on my tail. Instantly I hauled back on the stick and streaked upward. And just in time. For as I flicked into the climb, I saw the tracer streaks pass beneath me. As I turned I had a quick look around the the "office" [cockpit]. My fuel reserve was running out and I had only about a second's supply of ammunition left. I was certainly in no condition to take on two Messerschmitts. But they seemed no more eager than I was. Perhaps they were in the same position, for they turned away for home. I put my nose down and did likewise.

But there was a price to be paid, both in men and machines, for such valiant resistance. From July through October, the Germans lost 1733 aircraft, the RAF lost 915.

By mid-July invasion plans were ready. In early August all German Army leaves were canceled and, in September, Hitler had nearly 3000 invasion craft of all types poised in German, Dutch, Belgian, and French ports, ready for the cross-Channel invasion. But the Luftwaffe had not yet been able to gain its objectives. The RAF Fighter Command, though badly mauled, had not been swept from the skies, nor had its airdromes and ground installations been destroyed. In fact, the RAF and the Royal Navy were striking back, attacking the entire German invasion coast line, bombing and shelling landing craft, shipping and embarkation points. Allied ships continued to steam into British ports and were unloaded. Losses were considerable, but munitions, ships, and planes continued to come off assembly lines, and production was never critically damaged.

The Germans then made a strategic error. Instead of continuing to batter RAF fighters and their installations, they called a halt. RAF fighter reserves were depleted; had the Luftwaffe persisted in its onslaught, the Spitfires and Hurricanes might have been driven from the sky. With control of the air, the Luftwaffe might have crippled the Royal Navy, the RAF bombing squadrons, and cut off the shipping lifeline into British ports. Britain might have been brought to her knees, or the invasion of the island fortress made a matter of simply ferrying troops across the Channel.

But in September, Göring despaired of knocking out the RAF and unleashed the Luftwaffe on London instead. Perhaps this was because 40 per cent of British imports came through its port, or because by reducing the city to rubble, the Nazis thought they could break the British spirit. Mass daylight raid after mass daylight raid swept up the Thames Estuary and blasted the capital. Fire bombs and high explosives wracked the city until mid-November, hitting the poor in the East End especially hard. But, the same heavy losses which had made Göring turn from trying to destroy the RAF Fighter Command, turned him away from day raids on London. Though German aircraft production was more than enough to replace losses in aircraft, trained pilots, navigators and bombardiers were more difficult to replace. In November, therefore, the Luftwaffe switched to night bombing. Night after night it battered the city. People slept in the subways—the British tubes or underground—and in shelters. They were killed,

While the Royal Air Force exacted a price from the Luftwaffe which Göring clearly could not continue to pay indefinitely, the British dug air raid shelters (above) and stoutly refused Hitler the triumph he wanted most — the cracking of English morale. Some children were sent to the country or to Canada, but many more remained with their parents. Studies made after the war showed that those who stayed suffered less psychological damage than those away from home.

In September, Göring turned to terror raids against London. The RAF fighters

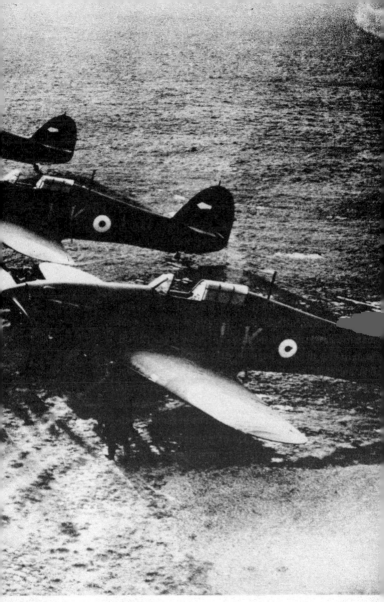

(above) knocked down two German planes for every English aircraft destroyed.

British planes on attack. Nazi bombers lacked long-range fighter cover.

crippled, and buried alive, but civilian heroism now equaled that of the RAF fighter pilots. Instead of faltering, British determination hardened. Londoners showed not only that they "could take it," but they went about their business with defiant fortitude. Ships were unloaded, factories continued to produce, and communications continued to be repaired and run. Ci-

Nightly, at the whine of the air raid sirens, the Londoners went to the under-

vilian air wardens spotted aircraft, fire watchers caught and fought fires from incendiary bombs, volunteers dug out those buried, the engineers defused and carried away unexploded and delayed-action bombs, and physicians and nurses tried to repair as much of the human damage as they could.

To the Germans it looked like victory. Gottfried

ground — the subway — to sleep as best they could while the battle raged.

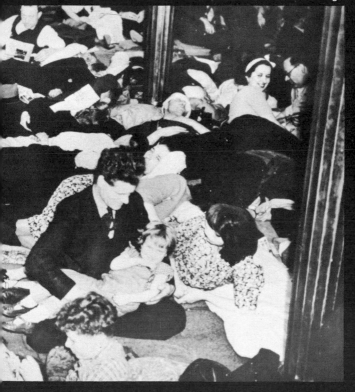

St. Paul's Cathedral sustained direct hits, but stood throughout the blitz.

Nearly a quarter of a million British were killed or wounded (above) during the German onslaught. Somehow, England continued to function. The rubble was pushed aside, the dud bombs removed (right) and by the end of 1940, Hitler had to admit the defeat. The Battle of Britain was over.

Leske, a Luftwaffe sergeant, wrote of the victory that was at hand:

This time we were to bomb the airdromes that ring London. We got into the ship, Lederer first, then Lommel, then Zoellner, then me, and then the Oberleutenant. There were twenty of us, including ourselves. Before and behind us were many tight sections of pursuit planes.

The air was soupy at 3000 meters, but it improves as we approached the Channel. We were in high spirits. We knew that today marked the beginning of the end. The long-awaited all-out attack on the heart of the British Empire had started. Today we would destroy the airdromes, power plants, hangars, and munitions depots and oil tanks of the enemy. Today we would smash England's defenses.

High above us our tough little ME's are flying. Al-

ready we are over Croydon, then over our target. It is shaped like a heart and lies close to a big highway. The JU's in front of us have already laid out their eggs. One of the hangars seems to have been hit, but otherwise they haven't done much damage.

But now the Hurricanes and Spitfires come diving down at us. In a moment they were whirling in dogfights with our chasers and destroyers. . . .

There were an awful lot of them there. I don't think they had more planes in the air than we did—probably they didn't—but they had nearly as many. And they had the advantage that they could land and refuel and come right back again, while our boys couldn't stay up there all the time because they were running out of gas. Our ME's darted about like hornets and more than one Hurricane dived vertically with glycol or cooling fluid pouring from it.

We finally managed to get rid of our packages. But Zoellner says he didn't think they did much good. Probably just made a few big holes in the field. Well, that's better than nothing. . . .

But I mustn't forget London. I saw it for the first time and I'll bet it will be the last time, too. It was during the second trip. The sky was cloudless, though with the dusk came a light mist. But I could still see the roofs of London. I saw the roofs of the city, which looks so irregular, almost disorderly, but in a way very colorful, and then I saw the broader and straighter suburban streets, and the Thames Estuary with its peculiar colors. I've tried to fix the picture in my mind, because I'm quite sure I'm one of the last men to have seen London. For a moment I thought it's really too bad that I've never been to London, and now never will be able to go there. Because today as I flew over this biggest city in the world, I knew with absolute certainty, as though I could foretell the future: This all will be destroyed. It will stand for but a few days more. Until the moment the Führer pronounces its death sentence. Then there will be nothing left but a heap of ruins.

These days are making history. And I am able to say that I participated. Ten or twenty years from now the history books will read: September 1940 — Destruction of London. The way we read about the destruction of Carthage. Or the burning of Rome.

London is burning. It is burning in a hundred places at the same time, and the whole city must be more a heap of ruins than a city. Again and again I think of my first flight over London, when none of our bombs had fallen upon it yet, when the greatest city in the world was still untouched and the English believed that no earthly power could possibly do anything to London. I imagine they've changed their minds about that by now.

Not a night passes without our setting new fires in the heart of the city — not a night when the sky doesn't become blood-red with the glow of flames. The flack fires, the searchlights light up the sky, but it does them no good. We won't quit, and we're doing a thorough job now. Yesterday it looked as though the Thames itself were burning. All the docks and warehouses were on fire, and every minute there were smaller explosions and bigger explosions. Over the whole city hangs a pall of dust and smoke. And still we keep at it, we never give them a breathing spell. Without any letup our formations fly over the city. It has been going on for a month now. London is dying....

But London refused to die. Though British fighters could do little against night bombers, the RAF Bomber Command retaliated against German cities. Berlin, Düs-

Britain struck back with heavy bombers. Air Marshal Sir Hugh Trenchard directed a systematic campaign of strategic night raids against German industrial might.

seldorf, Munich, Mannheim, Bremen, and other cities felt the weight of British bombs. The Nazis, in turn, hammered away at Britain's great industrial centers and major ports: Birmingham, Manchester, Leeds, Sheffield, Nottingham, Worcester, Bristol, Plymouth, Dover, and Southampton. On November 14, in one of the most ruthless bombings of the war, the small Midlands industrial city of Coventry was devastated. On December 29, a rain of Luftwaffe incendiaries set 1500 fires in London and the greatest blaze in London since the Great Fire of 1666. Almost 200,000 tons of bombs were dropped in the Battle of Britain, more than 40,000 civilians died and almost 200,000 were injured, but Britain stood fast. All over the free world there was horror at the indiscriminate bombing of civilians by the Nazis, and mounting admiration for British courage in the face of it.

Without command of the air, and with his navy still

crippled from the Norwegian campaign, Hitler decided to postpone the September 15 invasion deadline to October. In October he put it off until spring of 1941 when the weather would be better. Then he delayed it until after the Reich had beaten the Soviet Union. Finally, in January 1942, "Operation Sea Lion" was shelved altogether, but the invasion barges had long since been dispersed.

Though there has been much speculation on the subject, just why Hitler did not invade Britain still remains a riddle.

Britain's ordeal by fire was prolonged into the spring of 1941, when the bombing slacked off into sporadic raids, as Luftwaffe units were shifted to the Eastern Front to prepare for the coming battle in Russia. Since Hitler was mapping the assault on the Soviet Union, "Operation Barbarossa," in July 1940, and had already set May 1941 as the invasion date, why he went ahead with bombing Britain and preparing for its invasion remains unexplained. He may have thought that, after Dunkirk, Britain was a defenseless island and, like France, would collapse in six weeks after his September 15 invasion. Hitler might even have believed Göring's assurances that the Luftwaffe alone could bomb Britain to its knees. Or he might have considered that Britain would have little choice other than surrender once the Reich had defeated its last possible European ally, Russia. Certainly, the Führer disliked depending on Stalin for the torrents of grain, oil, and ores that the Russian leader had been shipping him.

Whatever the cause, Hitler's move on to the Russian steppes saved Britain and opened the two-front war which eventually was to bring his "Thousand Year Reich" down in ruins around his ears.

A grim Prime Minister Churchill walks through the ruins of Coventry.

Mediterranean Lifeline

When France fell, General Charles de Gaulle flew to England to fight on. Around him he gathered the Free French and established a provisional government in London, but neither France's North African nor Middle Eastern colonies rallied to his standard. Neither did the French Navy. Faced with the possibility that the Germans would take over the French Fleet, despite solemn Nazi pledges and French Admiral Jean Francois Darlan's guarantees, the British decided to take drastic action.

General Charles de Gaulle, who escaped from France to England where he

Without the French Fleet, blockade of Hitler's Europe was much more difficult and Britain's Mediterranean lifeline imperiled. Italy's entrance into the war had further tipped the balance of naval power. If the French Navy joined the Italian and German fleets, the Axis might have naval superiority over the British Fleet and so pave the way for invasion of England, or for cutting off British supply lines.

All this was further complicated by the increasing menace of Japanese naval might in the Far East and Japanese pressure on French Indochina and movements toward Singapore.

established the French National Committee, is seen inspecting his legions.

To supply their forces in Africa and the Middle East and to bring to England the oil without which the British war machine would sputter to a stop, the British had to keep the Mediterranean sea lanes open. The Royal Navy fought off aircraft and slugged it out when Italian surface units finally decided to venture forth. Reluctantly, it also smashed a French fleet at Oran (left), lest it fall into Axis hands and tip the balance of power.

The brilliant Admiral Sir Andrew Cunningham supported the desert campaign by using his battleships to bombard the Axis-held cities in Libya.

Britain struck at its former ally first. Fortunately, a large part of the French Navy was in British ports, at Plymouth and Portsmouth, and in Alexandria in Egypt. On July 3, 1940, the British quickly and almost bloodlessly seized those in England, and arranged for those in Egypt to be demilitarized. But major units of the French Fleet were in French North African ports — at Oran, Algiers, and Casablanca — and minor ones in Dakar, Madagascar, and Martinique. A British naval task force under Vice-Admiral Sir James F. Somerville

Cunningham, Britain's most brilliant sea dog since Nelson, smashed half the Italian Fleet at Taranto (right) with his carrier planes, then dodged in and out of heavy smoke to wallop it again in a slashing attack made off Cape Matapan.

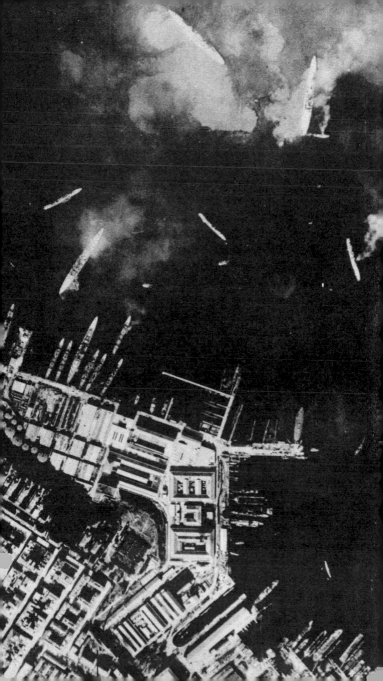

An outbound British convoy fights its way through dirty weather in the Bay of

was dispatched from Gibralter to Oran. There, the French commander, Vice-Admiral Marcel Gensoul, was given the choice of having his ships join the British, go to British ports, sail to Martinique and be demilitarized, or of scuttling them. If one of these choices was not acted upon within six hours, Somerville stated that he would regretfully have to use force to prevent the ships from falling into Axis hands.

Admiral Gensoul rejected the choices, and Somerville reluctantly attacked. Most of the French ships at Oran were sunk or disabled, and a thousand Frenchmen killed. One battle cruiser, the Strasbourg, and some minor units escaped to the French naval base at Toulon. Five days later, on July 8, British naval planes disabled the battleship Richelieu in Dakar, and left the battleship Jean Bart immobilized in Casablanca.

Biscay. In the spring of 1941, German submarines were winning the war at sea.

The following day the Vichy government broke off relations with the British government. A considerable French fleet was still based on Toulon and remained a threat in the Mediterranean. But, by unspoken agreement, the Germans never used those vessels, nor did the British use those interned in Alexandria, or those under American supervision in Martinique. Somerville's daring and ruthless stroke at Oran, so absolutely necessary to maintaining British naval superiority, eliminated the French as a major factor in the Mediterranean. The British now turned to the Italian Fleet.

In November 1940, Admiral Andrew Cunningham, commander of the British Eastern Mediterranean fleet, surprised the Italian Fleet in its Taranto naval base. At the price of only two aircraft lost, British naval planes put half the Italian Fleet out of commission.

47

In addition to the danger of submarines, convoy sailors had to sweat out the chances of collision, ever-present when large numbers of ships sail together blacked out at night (above). Near Europe (below), they also had to fight off raids by long-range Nazi bombers based in France and Norway.

Five months later, in protecting British convoys to Greece, Cunningham caught the Italian Fleet a second time off Cape Matapan in the Ionian Sea. He sank three cruisers, two destroyers, and damaged a considerable number of other ships. The Italian Fleet broke and fled for home. The balance of naval power in the Mediterranean had now definitely shifted to the British.

The Atlantic Lifeline

As part of the preparations for invasion of Britain, Hitler tried to blockade the embattled island. Cut off from the Continent, Britain was now more than ever dependent for survival on the resources of its Empire and the United States. Hitler was determined to sever that lifeline across the Atlantic from Canada and the Americas. The battle of the Atlantic was a combination of submarine warfare, surface raiding by heavy units of the German Navy, minelaying operations, and air attacks on shipping in British offshore waters.

The French surrender had made it easier for Hitler. French airfields were only minutes away from British coastal waters and ports. French submarine pens increased the range of German U-boats, so they could now operate far into the mid-Atlantic, beyond the protective radius of British planes. Hitler had French ports from which German minelayers could seed the Channel's waters, and French and Norwegian harbors from which German surface warships could suddenly appear to prey on British commerce in the North Atlantic.

After the fall of France the intensified U-boat campaign quickly doubled British merchant shipping losses. By May 1941 sinkings had mounted to a high of 500,000 tons for that month and a total of more than 7,000,000 tons sunk since the beginning of the war. For every

The submarine hunt was conducted by cruisers, destroyers, corvettes, PT boats, and planes. (Top, left) Captain F. J. Walker directing the final stages of a "kill." (Top, right) The wounded submarine breaks the surface of the water. (Bottom, left) Crewmen hover around the conning tower of their foundering craft. (Bottom, right) The Nazi crew has fled from the rapidly sinking U-boat. (Right) The bow of the submarine rears sharply before finally disappearing beneath the surface. But the peril to British merchant ships remained grave; and, slowly but surely, the battle of the Atlantic helped draw the United States into a more active role in the war.

ship coming down the ways of British and American shipyards, the Germans were sinking three. The situation was critical; either more boats had to be built, or the sinkings had to be stopped. Preferably both.

Against the U-boats, the most serious menace, the British adopted the convoy system worked out during World War I. This employed warships—battleships, cruisers, destroyers, PT boats, and corvettes—airplanes from small "baby" carriers, and land-based planes—from Greenland, Iceland, Northern Ireland, and the west coast of Britain—in combination to escort groups of merchant ships safely across the Atlantic.

But the work-horses of the convoy system were destroyers and patrol planes, both of which were in short supply. The RAF Coastal Command had been stripped of most of its planes to beef up the Fighter Command for the Battle of Britain, and many British destroyers had gone to the bottom in Norway, at Dunkirk, and in the routine patrolling of the sea lanes.

It was this battle of the Atlantic which slowly but surely drew the United States into the war.

In May 1940, with the threat of Italy's 100 submarines being joined to the Nazi U-boat fleet, and the fall of France imminent, Churchill asked President Roosevelt for 50 or 60 "obsolete" American destroyers and as many patrol planes as could be spared. Churchill was careful to emphasize that the British Fleet was America's first line of defense. If Britain lost control of the Atlantic, America's immediate interests were greatly in danger. After prolonged negotiations, FDR gave 50 "overage" destroyers to the British in September 1940 in exchange for 99-year leases on British bases in Newfoundland, the West Indies, and British Guiana. He did so in an executive agreement which required no Congressional endorsement.

Patrol planes (top, right) assisted the destroyers in combating the U-boats.

A signal man checks his iced-up blinker light (above) on a winter convoy in the Atlantic. (Below) A fortunate seaman naps between submarine alerts.

The Sinking of the Bismarck

While the U-boats struck silently from the deep, and the dive-bombers hit mostly at shipping in British coastal waters, German surface raiders went farther afield and inflicted heavy losses on British merchant shipping. In May 1941, the 45,000-ton German battleship Bismarck, pride of the German battle fleet, slipped out of its harbor in a fjord near Bergen, Norway, to prey on British convoys in the North Atlantic. It was accompanied by the light cruiser, Prinz Eugen, and a screen of destroyers.

British reconnaissance planes immediately spotted the flotilla and the British Admiralty sent a squadron, including the battleship Prince of Wales and the battle-cruiser Hood, racing to intercept. On the morning of May 24, they engaged off the coast of Greenland. The British ships were no match for the Bismarck's speed, armor, and accurate 15-inch-gun fire. In a matter of moments, the Hood was struck in the magazine and blown up. There were almost no survivors. The Prince of Wales, though it managed to hit the Bismarck, was itself damaged and forced to disengage.

Trying desperately to escape, the Bismarck steered swiftly for the French coastal port of Brest, hoping to find safe harbor there. The British Admiralty alerted every one of its ships in the area as far south as Gibralter, and the race was on. British orders were clear: find the Bismarck and sink it!

In a 2000-mile chase, the German superdreadnought was finally caught by a British squadron 400 miles from Brest. The Prinz Eugen and the rest of its escort ships had escaped. The Bismarck was left to face its pursuers alone.

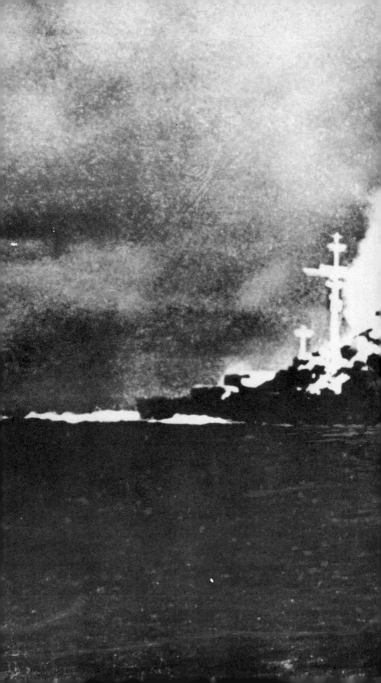

The Nazi battleship Bismarck firing in the action in which she sank the Hood.

On May 26, the Bismarck was attacked by the British battleships King George V and Rodney, shelled and torpedoed by their accompanying cruisers and destroyers, but fought back until Swordfish torpedo-bombers from the carriers Ark Royal and Victorious disabled its rudder and left it turning helplessly in the water. The next morning, the Bismarck was sunk by torpedoes from the cruiser Dorsetshire.

The War in Africa

Mussolini had long dreamed of a new Roman Empire built around the Mediterranean as an Italian lake. Annexation of Ethiopia in 1935, and its consolidation into an East African Empire with Eritrea and Italian Somaliland had been the first step. With France now out of the war, so that Mussolini was not threatened

British armor on the move in Africa. In 1940, British General Archibald Wavell

in the western Mediterranean and need deploy no troops against Vichy-controlled Tunisia, the Duce was ready for new imperial steps. His scheme for a new Rome and another mare nostrum was the defeat of the British Fleet in the Mediterranean, a thrust through Albania into Greece so he would control all of the north coast of the eastern Mediterranean, and finally an invasion of Egypt which would give him the southern coast, and the Suez Canal. The road to the Mosul Basin and Middle Eastern oil would then be open.

In August 1940 the first Italian army, under the viceroy of Ethiopia, the Duke of Aosta, struck north toward Egypt along the Blue Nile, threatening Khartoum in the Anglo-Egyptian Sudan. At the same time, Italian forces overran French and British Somaliland in two weeks. The next move was south into British Kenya.

The second army, under Marshal Rodolfo Graziani,

stopped an all-out Italian thrust, then counterattacked the larger enemy forces

struck east, the other arm of the pincers, from Libya. On September 13, Graziani sent his tanks and motorized divisions across the Egyptian border. Mussolini had prepared for his Libyan campaign for a long time. The Italians had built a 1000-mile road from Tripoli to the Egyptian border. All along the route, the seaports of Bengazi, Derna, Tobruk, Bardia, and Solum had been converted into supply bases for his armies. Not only did the Italians have overwhelming superiority of numbers — some 300,000 Italians against 70,000 British and Imperial troops — they also had more tanks, guns, anti-tank weapons, and planes.

Harried by light British forces who retreated toward Mersa Matruh, where the main British forces were, the Italians ground to a halt at Sidi Barrani and for three months stayed there. Mussolini finally had to threaten to remove Graziani from command to get the invasion

Supported by tanks, British infantry moves in open formation toward the en-

under way again.

But the British had not remained idle in the interim. In spite of the threat of Nazi invasion, Churchill had sent half of his best tanks from Britain and reinforced General Archibald Wavell's forces with Imperial troops from India, Australia, and New Zealand. Some South Africans and a Polish brigade were also added for good measure. On December 6, in a surprise attack, Wavell threw his new armored columns against the Italians. This was a different kind of warfare from that in France or in Flanders. Alan Moorehead, an English reporter with Wavell's forces, described it:

More and more I began to see that desert warfare resembled war at sea. Men moved by compass. No position was static. There were few if any forts to be held. Each truck or tank was as individual as a destroyer, and each squadron of tanks or guns made great

emy's lines. Reinforced RAF units provided Wavell with effective air cover.

The desert army included men from Great Britain, India, Australia, New Zealand

sweeps across the desert as a battle-squadron at sea will vanish over the horizon. One did not occupy the desert any more than one occupied the sea. One simply took up a position for a day or a week and patrolled it with Bren-gun carriers and light armoured vehicles. When you made contact with the enemy you manoeuvred about him for a place to strike much as two fleets will steam into position for action. There were no

and South Africa; here a few of them try to find cover from enemy shell fire.

trenches. There was no front line. We might patrol five hundred miles into Libya and call the country ours. The Italians might as easily have patrolled as far into the Egyptian desert without being seen. Actually these patrols in terms of territory meant nothing. They were simply designed to obtain information from personal observation and the capture of prisoners. And they had a certain value in keeping the enemy nervous. But

British Indian troops on the attack at Bardia during the Wavell offensive.

The successful British offensive cost the Italians more than 150,000 men in

always the essential governing principle was that desert forces must be mobile: they were seeking not the conquest of territory or positions but combat with the enemy. We hunted men, not land, as a warship will hunt another warship, and care nothing for the sea on which the action is fought. . . .

With air cover from reinforced RAF units, and aided by shelling from the Royal Navy, Wavell drove the Italians out of Egypt and across the fertile coastal strip of Cyrenaica. By February, his troops had taken Solum, Bardia, Tobruk, Derna, Bengazi, and finally halted at El Agheila on the border of Tripolitania. It was a tremendous victory and the end of Graziani's army. The

casualties and prisoners. Superior armor and brilliant tactics were decisive.

British had killed or captured more than 150,000 troops. Vast amounts of equipment were seized and more than two-thirds of the Italians' planes and ships were captured or destroyed. Nineteen Fascist generals were taken prisoner, or were "in the bag," as the British expression went. The British costs were less than 2000 casualties. Alan Moorehead, an eyewitness, almost could not believe it.

It was approaching Buq Buq that we came suddenly upon a sight that seemed at first too unreal, too wildly improbable to be believed. An entire captured division was marching back into captivity. A great column of dust turned pink by the sunset light behind them rose from the prisoners' feet as they plodded four abreast in the sand on either side of the metalled track. They came on, first in hundreds, then in thousands, until the stupendous crocodile of marching figures stretched away to either horizon. No one had time to count — six, possibly seven thousand, all in dusty green uniforms and cloth caps. Outnumbered roughly five hundred to one, a handful of British privates marched alongside the two columns and one or two Bren-gun carriers ran along the road in between. The Italians spoke to me quite freely when I called to them, but they were tired and dispirited beyond caring. I found no triumph in the scene — just the tragedy of hunger and defeat.

Wavell also opened the new year, 1941, with an offensive in East Africa. British columns drove into Eritrea from the east and into Ethiopia along the Blue Nile. Two other spearheads from Kenya charged east into Italian Somaliland and north into Ethiopia. A fifth British column came across the Gulf of Aden and went on to clear the Italians from British Somaliland.

Against the Duke of Aosta's more than 200,000 men, the British had only some 30,000 troops, plus native Ethiopian tribesmen, but they conducted the campaign with a daring and brilliance that made up for their numerical inferiority. In a spectacular series of offensives over four months, British armies took Eritrea, French, British, and Italian Somaliland, and overran most of Ethiopia. Addis Ababa, the capital, fell on April 6, and a month later Emperor Haile Selassie was restored to his throne. The remnants of the Italian forces, were surrendered by the Duke of Aosta on May 17. Most of the 200,000 Italian troops had been killed or captured; the Gulf of Aden and the Red Sea, route to Suez and the Mediterranean was cleared, and Mussolini's East African Empire lay shattered.

A tiny British force attacked south from Egypt towards Mussolini's newest African colony, Ethiopia. Fast moving columns (above) stalled temporarily before the heights at Keren, then swept ahead again after the 4th Indian Division stormed them. Haile Selassie (below) returned home triumphantly.

The United States: Arsenal of Democracy

For a long time, articulate American public opinion had been divided between isolationists and interventionists. The isolationists were opposed to United States involvement in foreign wars and entangling alliances. The interventionists believed that there was an identity of interests between America and those nations defending democracy against fascism.

The isolationists were a motley group of Americans who for varied reasons believed the war in Europe was not their war. Among them were native American fascists—Fritz Kuhn's German-American Bund, William Dudley Pelley's Silver Shirts, Christian Fronters, and Ku-Klux Klansmen—and Nazi and Fascist foreign agents. There were Communists following the "party line," which until June 1941 called the war a "bourgeois-imperialist" war—until the Nazis attacked the "Soviet motherland." There were pacifists, like Socialist Norman Thomas, who were simply anti-war, and the Irish, who simply and traditionally were anti-British. There were Italians and Germans who sympathized with the lands of their origin, or were enamored of Il Duce and Der Führer. Some were anti-New Deal and therefore against anything Franklin Roosevelt favored. Others were pro-New Deal, but did not want to divert American time, energy and money from domestic social reforms to armaments and resistance to aggression. Among isolationist leaders were Senators Burton K. Wheeler and Gerald P. Nye, newspaper tycoons Colonel Robert McCormick and William Randolph Hearst, and aviator Charles A. Lindbergh. Many of these groups and individuals rallied around the America First Committee, organized in September 1940.

In the critical summer of 1940, when France fell and England was left alone to face the Luftwaffe and perhaps Nazi invasion, American sentiment began to call for more effective aid to Britain. Quickly, the United States moved to help Britain and to help itself. In the summer of 1940, after most of Britain's arms had been abandoned on the littered beaches of Dunkirk, America sent 600,000 rifles, 900 field guns, and stocks of ammunition from surplus and obsolete stores to stave off the imminent Nazi invasion. Over the summer Congress began to appropriate billions of dollars to build a two-ocean navy, a huge air force, and a giant army. In August, joint planning with Canada, already fighting as one of the British Dominions, was begun. In September, FDR turned over the 50 "overage" American destroyers to fill the gap in the British Fleet, which now had half its destroyers out of commission. The Tri-Partite Pact between Germany, Italy, and Japan that same month quickened America's apprehension for its own security and hardened American determination. September also saw the first peacetime conscription passed by Congress. The Selective Service Act drafted for a year of military training all men between 21 and 36 years old. The intention was to provide an army of 1,200,000 and 800,000 reserves.

In the November Presidential elections that year, Roosevelt was elected for an unprecedented third term. Both he and the Republican candidate, Wendell Willkie, ran on foreign-policy slates of all-out aid to Britain.

In a post-election "fireside chat" on December 29, President Roosevelt told the American people and the world where the nation stood:

If Great Britain goes down, the Axis powers will control the continents of Europe, Asia, Africa, Australasia,

America was preparing to go to war, but some Americans did not like the idea. Above, Representative Clare Hoffman, Elizabeth Dilling and Frank Woodruff demonstrate against the draft. (Below) May Day marchers protest in New York.

Groups sympathetic to Hitler and Nazism sprang up around the country. (Above) Fritz Kuhn, the leader of the German-American Bund, speaks at a rally decked in Nazi trappings.

and the high seas — they will be in a position to bring enormous military and naval resources against this hemisphere. It is no exaggeration to say that all of us in the Americas would be living at the point of a gun — a gun loaded with explosive bullets, economic as well as military. . . . We must produce arms and ships with every energy and resource we can command. . . . We must be the great arsenal of democracy. . . .

The people of Europe who are defending themselves do not ask us to do their fighting. They ask us for the implements of war, the planes, the tanks, the guns, the freighters, which will enable them to fight for their liberty and our security. Emphatically we must get

73

Many patriotic Americans sincerely felt that the country had no vital interests at stake in the war. (Above) Senator Burton K. Wheeler, Charles A. Lindbergh, novelist Kathleen Norris and socialist Norman Thomas appear at an America First rally held in New York City to protest intervention.

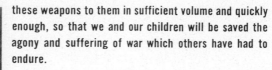

these weapons to them in sufficient volume and quickly enough, so that we and our children will be saved the agony and suffering of war which others have had to endure.

But a number of difficulties stood in the way of getting those planes, tanks, ships, and guns to Britain. In 1935, during the Italian invasion of Ethiopia, the U. S. Congress had passed a Neutrality Act, whose intention was to localize and isolate wars by denying arms and ammunition to the combatants. Whatever its intent, the legislation was invoked to the detriment of the Ethiopians and the Spanish Loyalist government when they fought against fascist aggression. In the Far East, the Japanese, in spite of the neutrality legislation, were permitted to buy the arms and raw materials they needed to carry out their conquest of China.

A few days after war began in September 1939, Roosevelt declared a limited national emergency and called for revision of the neutrality laws, which now denied the implements of war to the British and the French. Two months later, in November, Congress substituted a "cash-and-carry" scheme which permitted belligerents to buy arms for cash and carry them away in their own ships. Since Britain had the ships and the cash, this amendment to the neutrality legislation worked effectively in favor of the Allies.

If President Roosevelt had told the world what the nation was against in his December 29 speech, a week later, on January 6, 1941, he told the world what America was for:

In the future days, which we seek to make secure, we look forward to a world founded upon four essential freedoms.

The first is freedom of speech and expression— everywhere in the world.

The second is freedom of every person to worship God in his own way—everywhere in the world.

The third is freedom from want—which, translated into world terms, means economic understandings which will secure to every nation a healthy peacetime life for its inhabitants—everywhere in the world.

The fourth is freedom from fear—which translated into world terms, means a world-wide reduction of armaments to such a point and in such a thorough fashion that no nation will be in a position to commit an act of physical aggression against any neighbor—anywhere in the world.

But aggression was abroad in the world and Britain

American sailors explain our depth charges to British seamen sent over to

was fighting against it alone. As its assets shrank and U-boats and raiders took a mounting toll of its merchant shipping, cash and carry became impossible. British courage in the face of the blitz and Roosevelt's inspired leadership combined with an ebbing tide of isolationism to make America more eager and ready to help Britain get the materials to carry on, and to make the United States the "arsenal of democracy."

Three things were of first importance: money and credit; arms and munitions; and ships. In providing them, the U. S. moved quickly from neutrality to "nonbelligerence" to the brink of war. On March 11, 1941, Congress passed the "Lend-Lease" Act.

pick up the 50 old destroyers given to England to help fight submarines.

Secretary of War Stimson, blindfolded, draws the first draft number. All

In explaining to a press conference what Lend-Lease was, President Roosevelt used a homely image:

Suppose my neighbor's house catches fire and I have a length of garden hose four or five hundred feet away. If he can take my garden hose and connect it up with his hydrant, I may help him to put out the fire. Now what do I do? I don't say to him before that operation, "Neighbor, my garden hose cost me fifteen dollars; you have to pay me fifteen dollars for it." No! What is the transaction that goes on? I don't want fifteen dollars — I want my garden hose back after the fire is over.

The new act empowered the President to lend or lease American materials and facilities to any nation whose defense he considered essential to the United States' security, and it appropriated $7,000,000,000 to get the program under way. And now ships, planes, tanks, and guns could be sent to Britain without payment. The next step was to help them get there.

This was all-out aid short of war. In March, the same month Lend-Lease was passed, the U. S. seized all Axis shipping in American ports. In April, American naval units began a "neutrality patrol" to guard convoys to the British Isles up to the "war zone." That zone was arbitrarily defined as halfway across the Atlantic. This tactic relieved the pressure on the British Navy which now only had to provide escorts for the western half of the ocean. In May, Roosevelt declared an unlimited national emergency. The same month the U. S. agreed to train 8000 British pilots a year. In June, the American government froze Axis assets and expelled the Axis consular, press, and tourist organizations. In July and August, American troops relieved British and Canadian forces on Greenland and Iceland, and took over the defense of both countries.

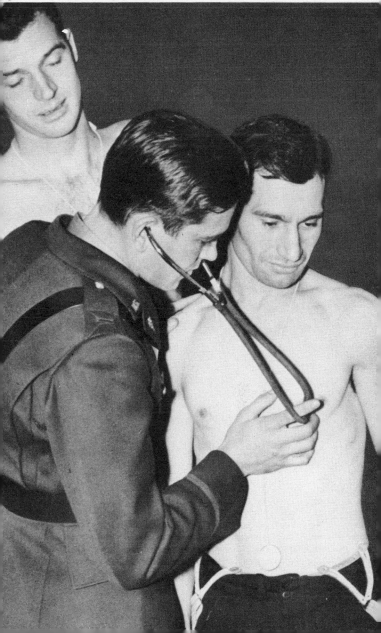

The new draftees looked about as sorry as rookies always do, but soon . . .

some were on duty in Iceland.

The Germans retaliated swiftly. Three U.S. destroyers on "neutrality patrol" were torpedoed. In September, Roosevelt ordered American naval vessels to attack Axis warships in American "defense areas." In November, Congress permitted merchant ships to be armed and allowed them into combat zones. If daily the United States moved inexorably closer to war, it now did so with the understanding that Roosevelt had embodied in an address on May 27:

Nobody can foretell tonight just when the acts of the dictators will ripen into attack on this hemisphere and us. But we know enough by now to realize that it would be suicide to wait until they are in our front yard.

When your enemy comes at you in a tank or a bombing plane, if you hold your fire until you see the whites of his eyes, you will never know what hit you. Our Bunker Hill of tomorrow may be several thousand miles from Boston ...

There are some timid ones among us who say that we must preserve peace at any price — lest we lose our liberties forever. To them I say: Never in the history of the world has a nation lost its democracy by a successful struggle to defend its democracy. We must not be defeated by the fear of the very danger which we are preparing to resist. Our freedom has shown its ability to survive war, but it would never survive surrender. The only thing we have to fear is fear itself.

The Atlantic Charter

On August 9, 1941, a little more than two months later and some six weeks after the Nazis invaded the USSR, Anglo-American cooperation was dramatically reaffirmed by a secret meeting between Churchill and Roosevelt at Placentia Bay, Newfoundland. Their purpose was to proclaim publicly the guiding principles of democratic policy. Simultaneously, and perhaps more important, the President and the Prime Minister and their staffs conferred on the crucial problems facing them: supplies to Britain, the battle of the Atlantic, aid to newly invaded Russia, and the mounting threat of Japanese aggression in the Far East. Though care was taken not to make commitments other than those authorized by the Congress, a joint declaration called the Atlantic Charter was issued on August 12:

The President of the United States of America and the Prime Minister, Mr. Churchill, representing His Majesty's Government in the United Kingdom, being met together, deem it right to make known certain common principles in the national policies of their respective countries on which they base their hopes for a better future for the world.

First, their countries seek no aggrandizement, territorial or other.

Second, they desire to see no territorial changes that do not accord with the freely expressed wishes of the people concerned.

Third, they respect the right of all peoples to choose the form of government under which they will live; and they wish to see sovereign rights and self-government restored to those who have been forcibly deprived of them.

Fourth, they will endeavor, with due respect for their existing obligations, to further the enjoyment by all States, great or small, victor or vanquished, of access, on equal terms, to the trade and to the raw materials of the world which are needed for their economic prosperity.

Fifth, they desire to bring about the fullest collaboration between all nations in the economic field, with the

object of securing for all improved labor standards, economic advancement, and social security.

Sixth, after the final destruction of the Nazi tyranny they hope to see established a peace which will afford to all nations the means of dwelling safety within their own boundaries, and which will afford assurance that all the men in all the lands may live out their lives in freedom from fear and want.

Seventh, such a peace should enable all men to traverse the high seas and oceans without hindrance.

Eighth, they believe that all the nations of the world, for realistic as well as spiritual reasons, must come to the abandonment of the use of force. Since no future

President Roosevelt and Prime Minister Churchill during divine services on the

peace can be maintained if land, sea, or air armaments continue to be employed by nations which threaten, or may threaten, aggression outside of their frontiers, they believe, pending the establishment of a wider and permanent system of general security, that the disarmament of such nation is essential. They will likewise aid and encourage all other practicable measures which will lighten for peace-loving peoples the crushing burden of armaments.

The joint declaration was soon subscribed to by the Soviet Union and nine governments-in-exile, and gave encouragement to all who were resisting aggression in the dark days of 1941.

U.S. cruiser Augusta during the Atlantic Charter meeting held in Newfoundland.

Mediterranean Blitzkrieg

War in the Balkans

In fall 1940, Mussolini was still looking forward to victories in Egypt and East Africa. To show his independence of his partner-in-aggression, and to protect his own imperial designs in the Balkans, Il Duce sent 200,000 troops hurtling across the Albanian border into Greece on October 28. Greece was small and weak. Virtually without planes, tanks, armor, or heavy guns, Greece could only oppose 16 divisions to Mussolini's 27, and Il Duce was sure his victory would rival the blitzkrieg successes of his Axis ally. Italian columns plunged through the Pindus Mountain valleys and into the Epirus, thrusting toward Yanina. But the Greeks pounded them from the mountainsides, inflicting heavy losses on the Italians, and stopped them. Within three weeks Greek counterattacks had driven the Italian spearheads back across the border into Albania. On November 21, the Greeks seized the chief Italian supply depot in northern Macedonia, Koritza, and on December 8, the major Italian jumping-off base in southern Albania, Argyrokastron. By the end of the year, only two months after the campaign had so confidently been launched, the Greeks had pushed the Italian legions forty miles back into Albania on a broad front and had brought more than a quarter of Albania under their control.

In preparing to invade Russia, Hitler had been consolidating his power that fall and winter and had coerced Hungary, Romania and Bulgaria into joining the Axis. Mussolini's independent attack on Greece endangered all his plans. It revived old border and nationalities quarrels among his new junior partners. It was sure to bring British troops to aid the Greeks. And it was bound to make the already uneasy Russians even

Italians advancing in Greece. The stubborn Greeks proved too much for them.

more suspicious of Axis designs on the Balkans. But once Il Duce's columns had been halted, Hitler had to come to Italy's aid. He had to protect Axis prestige and secure his flank before he invaded Russia.

Hitler preferred to do this through diplomacy, if he could, reserving his military strength for the campaign against the USSR. To strike more easily at Greece, he tried to bring the Yugoslavs into the Axis by guaranteeing their borders and offering them the Greek port of Salonika as booty if they would "cooperate." Pro-Nazi Regent Prince Paul and Prime Minister Cvetkovich were agreeable. They signed the Tri-Partite Pact on March 25, 1941, but two days later their government was overthrown and the agreement repudiated. Popular demonstrations against collaboration with the Nazis had given air force General Dusan Simovitch his chance for a coup. He took it, assumed the reins of government, and replaced the Regent with young King Peter.

Ten days later, on April 6, after swiftly improvising a plan of a campaign, Hitler sent the Wehrmacht sweeping into Yugoslavia and Greece. In a ruthless and rapid blitzkrieg 650,000 troops moved into Yugoslavia from four directions. Nazi spearheads from Austria, Hungary, Romania, and Bulgaria cut the bewildered and ill-equipped Yugoslav Army to shreds. On April 17, only 11 days later, it was forced to surrender. King Peter fled to England, and the largest of the Balkan countries, with 14,000,000 inhabitants and 95,000 square miles, was in German hands.

For Belgrade, the Yugoslav capital, Hitler had a special sadistic fate in store. Though it had been declared an open city, he had the Luftwaffe bomb it unmercifully in what he called "Operation Punishment"—punishment for having repudiated the Axis. In low-level bombing attacks, the unopposed German bombers

Wearing traditional uniforms, heroic Greek evzones march through Athens.

Though weak in artillery (above) and troops (below), Greece put up strong resistance and counterattacked in the mountains along the Albanian border.

rained death down on Belgrade and killed 17,000 of its citizens. Robert St. John, an American newsman, recorded the horror.

We heard the planes before we saw them. At first it was just a faint drone. Like a swarm of bees a long way off. Then louder. Louder! LOUDER!... Thirty or forty of them! What a perfect formation! But why aren't there any Yugoslav fighters up there heading them off. Look, they're coming right at us! Right at the Srpski Kralj!

All at once a million machine guns began talking.... That deep-throated booming must be from Yugoslav pom-poms. We knew the next noise came from ack-ack guns. A dozen of them must have gone off all at the

Belgrade, Yugoslavia, was destroyed by a brutal Nazi air raid during which 17,000 lost their lives (below). Once inside the country, the Germans opened a repressive campaign against civilians and partisans (right) which made the Yugoslavian experience one of the bitterest of the occupied countries.

same time. Now the sky was full of black and white puffs. They looked like little clouds. Then they disintegrated. That was shrapnel from the ack-ack guns. Some of the stuff was pretty close to the bombers, but the bombers didn't stop. They didn't even get out of formation. . . . They must have been flying at ten thousand feet. All at once they broke formation. The leader went into a fast dive. We could tell about where he dropped his first bombs. Then the dull thuddy sound. And in a couple of seconds we heard the thick noise walls make when they fall into the street in pieces. . . .

Back in the square we saw one place where a bomb had made a hole in the street big enough to bury a couple of railroad cars. I mean big American railroad cars. We walked up as close as we could to it, but still we couldn't see down to the bottom. You never saw such a mess as Terrazia was. I don't think there was a piece of glass more than a few inches square within half a mile. The bombs had torn the fronts right off a lot of buildings. I know that's old stuff. Everyone's seen pictures of buildings like that in Spain and in France and Rotterdam and, of course, in London. But it was different seeing it right in front of your eyes. Especially when the bombers were still over your head and you didn't know if they were through with the job or not. Those naked buildings made us think of Eugene O'Neill's Desire under the Elms, where they had a house on the stage and took away parts of the front wall so you could see what went on inside. . . .

We counted two or three hundred bodies right in Terrazia, and Terrazia isn't half as big as Times Square. Terrazia proved to me that this was all intentional. These planes that were bombing Belgrade had everything their own way. They weren't releasing bombs from up in the clouds. Every one of them came down in a dive or a glide and planted his bombs just where the crew wanted to plant them. From what we saw in Belgrade that day we decided they could have dropped a bomb right down the flue of a chimney, their aiming was so accurate. There wasn't any mystery about why Terrazia was one of the "military objectives" they hit, as Berlin called them in the communiques after it was all over. Hitler was getting his revenge for the humiliation of ten days ago. He was showing the Serbs that no one could tear up his picture in public and get away with it.

This was a mass execution of the guilty, of those who had demonstrated in Terrazia.

It was a mass execution carried out on orders from Berlin, with the executioners riding the clouds. . . .

About ten miles from Belgrade there was a spot where the highway circled around a hill. When we got up there we could get a good view of the whole scene. Behind us we could see Belgrade. Burning Belgrade. Belgrade already well on the way to becoming a city of silent people. . . .

Swastika Over the Acropolis

On April 6, the same day Hitler attacked Yugoslavia, from Bulgaria and Yugoslavia, German armor sliced south into Greece. Nazi spearheads were quickly joined to the faltering Italian divisions and the Greek armies were driven back.

Only a week after Mussolini invaded Greece, on November 8, British and Imperial troops, chiefly Australian and New Zealanders, had begun to land in Greece to reinforce the Greek Army. To do so, the British had to strip Wavell's army in North Africa, forcing it to halt its victorious march at El Agheila. Some 60,000 of

Wavell's men, half his army, had been sent to Greece. It was too little, too late. From a military point of view they were too few to hold back the 500,000 Nazi troops, and they had almost no armor, anti-tank weapons, or airplanes. But with a political eye on the Middle East, Churchill said, "No doubt our prestige will suffer if we are ignominiously ejected, but in any event to have fought and suffered in Greece would be less damaging to us than to have left Greece to her fate."

As its major defense lines — the Metaxas and Aliakhmon lines — were outflanked and pierced, the Greek Army crumbled in the face of the Nazi assault. With superiority in men and ten planes to every Allied one, Nazi columns quickly drove a wedge between the Greeks and the British and Imperial forces, and the Greek Army was forced the surrender. The British retreated, fighting dogged and valiant rear-guard actions.

Only eighteen days after the campaign began, the Greek Army surrendered on April 24, but not before telling their British and Imperial allies to evacuate and save the country from further destruction. A new Dunkirk began from the harbors and beaches of southern Greece. From Piraeus, Nauplion, Megara, Monemvasia, and other ports, the British rescued more than 80 per cent of their troops. By May 2, as Nazi columns reached the shore, the British had re-embarked more than 43,000 men. Naval intervention by the Italians had been forestalled by Admiral Cunningham's brilliant defeat of the Italian fleet off Cape Matapan on March 28, but the Luftwaffe took a heavy toll of 26 British ships.

Hitler divided the spoils among his allies. An "independent" Croatia was set up under native fascists Ante Pavelitch and Sladko Kvaternik. Hungary received the Banat, Bulgaria got Thrace, and Italy was awarded the Adriatic Coast and the unpleasant job of policing the

Germans man a 20 mm anti-aircraft gun mounted on a tractor-truck.

Rough terrain in northern Greece failed to hold up the Germans for long

new Greek puppet state under General George Tsolakoglou. The minor award to Italy symbolized the change in its role in the Axis. Having once pulled Mussolini's chestnuts out of the Greek fire, Hitler gradually reduced Italy to another Axis satellite.

Debacle in Crete

There was almost no pause in German operations. The Luftwaffe began to bomb the island of Crete and the Suez Canal in preparation for the first airborne invasion of the war. Though the British had had a half year to prepare Crete against invasion, not much had been done. There were too few airfields accommodating too few planes, and almost no anti-aircraft guns. Now the Germans gave the British no breathing space. In mounting tempo, German bombers blasted the island's defenses, concentrating on the three airfields and the places parachutists and glider-borne infantry were to land. When these were softened up, parachute assault troops were dropped to hold the positions until glider and airborne troops could be landed to back them. The paratroops seized and held the essential Maleme airdrome against counterattacks while the Nazis poured a flood of airborne reinforcements on the airport into the battle for Crete. The invasion from the air began on May 20 and this is what it looked like to Greek doctor, Theodore Stephanides, who was attached to the British forces:

May 20th dawned bright and fine. At about 7:30 A.M. some of the other officers and I were standing near the mess tent, chatting and waiting for breakfast to be served, when suddenly without any warning there was a terrific burst of ack-ack fire. We all sprang into the slit-trenches, thinking that this was just another of

With Nazi armor racing over the ground and parachutists dropping from the sky, the fall of Greece could not be long delayed. A game British force was ferried up from Africa to help out, but it lacked the heavy arms to do more than stall the advance. The British Navy took the men out again.

The German paratroopers who took Crete after bombers blasted the island

the ordinary raids we had got so used to lately. But
this time it was something very different. Before we
knew what was happening, the skies were full of
German planes which had apparently sprung from nowhere. There seemed to be hundreds of them, diving,
zooming, and criss-crossing as they bombed and ma-
chine-gunned all over the place. Then a flight of large
silvery machines passed low down over our heads,
coming from the southwest and making for Canea. They
passed as silently as ghosts with just a swishing sound
instead of the usual roar, and their wings were very
long and tapering. It was only then that I understood
that these were gliders and that an airborne attack on
Crete had begun in grim earnest.

The amazing Admiral Cunningham took his fleet in to evacuate British troops on Crete. Though he knew in advance that the operation would cost him badly-needed ships — and it did — Cunningham went in doggedly (above) and managed to bring off more than half the force. Many others (below) were imprisoned. British morale sank to its lowest since Dunkirk.

Shells from our ack-ack guns were bursting all around the gliders and their accompanying planes, but these were so many and our guns so pitifully few that little damage seemed to be caused. I saw one glider twist sideways with a jerk and come down behind the trees at a very steep slant, and I guessed that it must have crashed, but most of the others—about thirty, I estimated—slid serenely on and descended in the direction of Canea. They were going much slower than an ordinary plane and I reflected what a hash a few of our Hurricanes would have made of them if only they had been there.

I was just gazing at a bomber which appeared to have been hit, as it was swaying from side to side with a long plume of black smoke trailing behind it, when there was a shout from Captain Fenn: 'Look! Parachutists!'

I spun around and saw a row of tiny black dots falling from some of the planes which were buzzing around. They seemed to have been loosed from a very low altitude, and they blossomed out almost instantly into little white umbrellas which disappeared behind the trees. Some of the parachutes appeared to be coloured, green or brown, but they were too far away (luckily!) for me to be certain. Some again were much larger than the others and had a curious elongated shape; it was only later that I learnt that these were triple parachutes carrying light mortars, munitions, and other heavy stuff. The planes weaved continuously in all directions and dropped wave after wave of these parachutes in a long arc extending from roughly south-west to north of us. . . .

Without air cover and exposed to merciless Luftwaffe bombing and strafing, British and Imperial troops were nonetheless able to wreak havoc among the Nazi parachute and airborne assault forces. In an attempt to avoid these heavy casualties, the Germans tried to slip three small-boat convoys through the British naval blockade to reinforce their troops on Crete. But Admiral Cunningham's Eastern Mediterranean fleet caught them, routed one and destroyed two, with more than 5000 German casualties resulting. But the Nazis, in spite of losses at sea and the heavy toll taken among their parachute and glider troops, relentlessly poured airborne reinforcements into the beleaguered island through strategic Maleme airfield.

Soon German dominance began to tell. Fighting their by now habitual and valiant rear-guard actions, British and Imperial troops wearily retreated to the open beaches at Sphakia, on the southwestern coast of Crete, for another Dunkirk. From here, between May 28 and June 1, the Royal Navy wrought another miracle and brought out 16,500 troops, though 13,000 dead, wounded, and prisoners were left behind. Without air cover in Cretan coastal waters or over the 350 miles of Mediterranean to Suez, the Navy also sustained more than 2000 casualties and lost 3 cruisers, 4 destroyers, and many smaller craft to the Luftwaffe. The German Air Force also managed to damage 1 battleship, 2 cruisers, and 4 destroyers, seriously weakening the Eastern Mediterranean fleet.

In two months the Nazis had taken all Yugoslavia and Greece at small cost. They had only slightly more than 2500 killed and some 9000 missing and wounded. For victory in Crete they paid a good deal more, with 17,000 casualties and heavy losses in aircraft. But now they controlled the Aegean Sea, and threatened the East Mediterranean and Cunningham's debilitated British Fleet there. They were also within striking distance of Turkey, Egypt, and the Middle East. With the Balkans

General Erwin Rommel who was sent to manage the Axis campaign in Africa.

secured in less than two months, Hitler could now turn his attention to his invasion of Russia.

Had Hitler then thrown his armies against the Middle East, instead of against the USSR, the course of the war might have been drastically altered. Instead, in April and May, while Nazi legions charged through Yugoslavia, Greece, and Crete, Axis agents working with the Vichy French tried to seize control of the vital area by pro-Axis coups in Iraq, Syria, and Iran. Control of those countries would have deprived the British of their crucial oil supplies and have isolated Turkey, probably forcing it into the Axis camp. It would also have threatened India with invasion from the west and eliminated the supply route to Russia through the Persian Gulf and Iran. In June, British and Free French forces swiftly seized Syria and Iraq, ousted the Axis partisans, and installed pro-Allied governments. In August, after the Nazis had invaded Russia, Britain and the USSR partitioned Iran, replaced its pro-Nazi government and thus secured the Iranian supply route.

Enter the Desert Fox

As Hitler increasingly took control of the war in the Mediterranean from Mussolini, the picture there darkened for the British. In January 1941, Luftwaffe units were sent to Sicily and their bombers soon made the narrow straits between Sicily and Cape Bon in Africa virtually impassable. Heavy losses were inflicted on British convoys and naval units trying to go through the central Mediterranean. Malta, the British bastion which had· given air cover to those convoys, was bombed several times daily, reducing its effectiveness and limiting the reinforcements that could be gotten through to the island for its own defense.

Two weeks after he arrived in Africa, Rommel launched an offensive.

The desert provided little cover for either side against air attacks. But now with complete command of the air, Rommel could blast the British at will. (Above) A supply column is hit; (below) infantrymen take cover.

But most important, in February, German General Erwin Rommel, one of the Wehrmacht's best tank tacticians, was put in charge of a unified command of all Axis forces in the Western desert, including his own specially trained desert warriors, the Afrika Korps. Rommel was a daring and unorthodox fighter who understood the essentials of desert mobile warfare. Here, Chester Wilmot, Australian historian and reporter, tells what those essentials were:

Burnt-out and blasted equipment littered the desert around Tobruk.

Two main considerations governed warfare in the Libyan-Egyptian desert: supply, and the balance of 'mobile striking power' — a term which may be used to cover the combined power of tanks, anti-tank guns and field artillery working together as a common force. The chief geographical factor influencing tactics in this desert is that, except at El Alamein near Alexandria and at El Agheila on the border of Tripolitania, there are no defensive positions that cannot be outflanked. At both these places secure flanks are provided by narrow bottlenecks — between the Mediterranean and the Qattara Depression in one case, and the Great Sand Sea in the other Everywhere else there is an open desert flank, the cause of constant anxiety to the commander who has not superiority in mobile striking power. Even the most gallant infantry cannot hold fixed positions in this desert when once enemy armoured forces have outflanked them. Then, if they are not to be cut off, they must withdraw and keep on withdrawing until wear and tear or supply difficulties reduce the enemy's superiority in armoured and mobile forces to such an extent that he loses control of the open desert flank. Their only alternative is to establish themselves behind a fortified perimeter covering a water-point and harbour like that at Tobruk.

Ignoring the advice of the German General Staff, which was about to begin its invasion of the Balkans, Rommel, only two weeks after he had arrived in Africa, launched a surprise attack on British positions at El Agheila on March 31. The British, weakened by the withdrawal of half their troops to Greece, gave ground. Rommel, with command of the air in his hands, pressed hard on their heels, outflanked, outmaneuvered, and outfought the forces facing him. A spearhead of his motorcyclists cut into a retreating British column and captured two British Generals — Lieutenant-Generals Richard O'Connor and Philip Neame. Within two weeks, he had driven the British back to the Egyptian frontier, and retaken all of Cyrenaica up to and including Bardia, with the exception of bypassed and besieged Tobruk.

Eric Lambert, a British observer, portrayed the rout:

Vehicles shouldered each other crazily on the crammed roadway. To keep fleeing was the only thought. Some of the battered transport broke down and was abandoned. Some of the division were overtaken and made prisoner. In Nazi prison camps Australians came to talk of the 'Breakfast Battalion.' Its commander, perhaps under the delusion that he was still engaged in leisurely maneuvering with his militia company somewhere back in Australia, ordered the battalion to 'stop for breakfast.' His officers demurred, pointing out that the Nazi scout cars were only a few miles away. The colonel repeated serenely that 'the battalion would stop for breakfast.' Those of the companies who could manage it disobeyed and kept on fleeing. The colonel and about a hundred of his men stopped for breakfast. For the next four years they partook of that meal in Nazi prison camps: a long time to stop for breakfast.

The tide had turned against the impudent force that occupied Cyrenaica. Rommel recaptured Benghazi. Six days after, 9 Division and the remnants of a British armoured division reached Tobruk. The Benghazi Derby was over. In Tobruk they turned to stand before Rommel and all that he had to hurl against them.

British and Australian forces holed up in Tobruk were now cut off from Egypt. Rommel threw attack after attack at the 23,000-man garrison, but he could not crack its semicircular perimeter. The city was shelled, dive-bombed, and assaulted by tanks, but the

Though Wavell was able to mount a counterattack on May 15, the Nazis had built up dominance on the ground. Their tanks were better than the British armor (below) and their 88 mm anti-tank gun was a genuinely outstanding weapon.

An artillery barrage lights up the horizon during a night battle in the desert.

Rommel struck back while half the British forces were still in Crete. He won

defenses held. Nor did the troops remain solely on the defensive. Time and again, the patrols struck at Nazi lines of supply and communication. They were an ever-present threat to Rommel's flank and rear. Despite fierce Luftwaffe air attacks, the Royal Navy managed to get its ships through to the besieged fortress during the nine-month siege. Reinforcements, arms, and ammunition, as well as food, were brought in, usually by fast destroyers and minelayers on moonless nights, and the wounded taken out.

Before the heat of the summer made operations almost impossible in the desert, Wavell launched a

a solid victory, took more prisoners (above), and drove Wavell back into Egypt.

counteroffensive on May 15. His armor and tank strength were inferior both in quantity and quality to Rommel's, and after small gains, he was thrown back to the Egyptian border. Churchill knew that the crucial battle for Egypt and the Suez Canal would soon have to be fought. He wanted Rommel crushed before reinforcements from the Russian front could be diverted to the Afrika Korps and break through Alexandria and Suez. On July 2, therefore, he replaced General Wavell with General Sir Claude Auchinleck. The Army of the Nile became the famous Eighth Army, and preparations were made for a major offensive against Rommel in the fall.

125

Rudolph Hess (above, with Hitler and Baldur von Schirach in 1938) had been one of the Führer's most fanatical lieutenants. Accordingly, it was a vast shock to Germany when Hess flew to Scotland, ostensibly to urge the British to fight against Russia. The British promptly interned him.

Hess: The Flying Dutchman

One of the stranger preludes to "Operation Barba-rossa," Hitler's plan for invading Russia, came a month before the campaign actually began. Rudolf Hess, third man in the Nazi hierarchy made a daring flight to England on May 10. He bailed out in a Scottish field only a little way from his goal, Dunvagel, where the Duke of Hamilton had an estate.

Hess had met the Duke at the 1936 Olympic Games in Berlin and looked on him as pro-Nazi. Through him, Hess hoped to persuade the King to bring about an agreement with Germany.

In parachuting to the ground, Hess fractured his ankle and was taken prisoner by a farmer who turned him over to the authorities. After interrogation, it was apparent that Hess's avowed purpose was to end hostilities between Germany and Britain — "racially Aryan brothers" — and to have Britain join Germany in a war against Bolshevism. Because he was certain of German victory, and sure that Britain's military position was hopeless, Hess's terms, by his lights, were not excessive. If Britain acceded to a free hand in Europe for Germany, returned Germany's colonies, made peace with Italy, and, finally, ousted the Churchill government, Hitler would leave Britain its Empire.

Hitler immediately denounced Hess's flight as the idealism of an unbalanced man suffering hallucinations, though, only six weeks later, on the very day Nazi Panzers rolled into Russia, his Ambassador to Turkey, the old conspirator Franz von Papen, put out similar peace feelers to the British Ambassador at Ankara.

The British treated Hess generously, as a mentally and physically sick man, but they refused to make terms with the Nazi "New Order."

127

Drive Toward the East

"Operation Barbarossa": The Invasion of Russia

In the summer of 1940, while the Nazis gathered invasion barges to strike at England, Hitler decided to conquer Russia. Why he made the decision then remains unknown. Had he thrown his armies into the Middle East, or sent them plunging through Spain and Gibraltar into North Africa, or reinforced the Italian drive on Suez from Libya, as his generals and admirals advised, he might have been victorious over Britain by cutting its lifelines. Perhaps he was sure Britain could be brought to terms, or that his "crusade against Bolshevism" would so appeal to right-wing anti-Communist groups and so divide opinion in Britain and the U.S., that both countries would not only accept Nazi conquest of Russia, but collaborate with it. What does seem to have motivated Hitler, when, in August 1940, he gave orders to prepare the invasion plans was his own intense hatred of Bolshevism, his distrust of Russia's age-old expansionist designs on Europe, especially on the Balkans, and his own frequently expressed desire, in the Ludendorff tradition, to seize Lebensraum living space, labor and raw materials in a Drang nach Osten (drive toward the East).

Though Hitler's suspicions of Soviet intentions were heightened by Stalin's seizure of Bessarabia and northern Bukovina from Romania and his annexation of the Baltic countries, both in June 1940, while the Führer's eyes were riveted on the fall of France, there was little evidence of Soviet intention to move west then. Since the Molotov-Ribbentrop Pact, the Soviets had, even by Hitler's standards, proved loyal allies and given him valuable political and economic support. Stalin had

Dr. Joseph Goebbels broadcasts Hitler's declaration of war against Russia.

sent Hitler 1,000,000 tons of grain, 500,000 tons each of iron ore and phosphates, and more than 900,000 tons of oil. The Soviets had even acted as agents for Germany in buying essential supplies from other countries, and had transported them to the Reich from the East, thus evading the British naval blockade. And Stalin was willing to do even more. Count von Schulenburg, German Ambassador to Moscow, assured Hitler that the Soviet dictator would give them up to 5,000,000 tons of grain a year. These raw materials were so important to Hitler that he put a priority on German shipments to the USSR even over deliveries to

German troops moving up during the early days of the Russian campaign. They moved ahead rapidly in spite of heavy Russian troop concentrations near the frontier. Russian armor was no match for the excellent Nazi tanks.

the German armed forces. The Russians remained so faithful and trusting that they sent materials right up to the invasion.

Politically, the Russians and their Communist Party puppets abroad had reinforced Nazi propaganda and "peace" offensives, dubbing the war a "bourgeois-imperialist" struggle, and blaming the Allies for beginning and continuing the war. Stalin maintained this political allegiance to Hitler right up to the very last moment too. In May 1941, only a month before the invasion, he retracted his recognition of the Belgian, Norwegian, and Yugoslav governments-in-exile, and accorded his recognition to the pro-Nazi Iraqi government.

Militarily, the Russians showed a marked indifference to the elimination of France from the war and the destruction of the possibilities of a Balkan front against Hitler, the "second front" they were soon to be clamoring for so stridently. Moreover, they wasted no pity on British suffering under the blitz, and showed a studied unconcern for the menace of German invasion of the British Isles.

The Tri-Partite Pact between Germany, Italy, and Japan, signed in September 1940, left the USSR out and Stalin wanted to know where the Soviet Union fitted into the Triplice and the New Order. Nazi moves into the Balkans, particularly Hitler's guarantee of Romania's borders, also displeased the Russians. Though they already had Bessarabia and northern Bukovina, they still coveted southern Bukovina. In mid-November Molotov came to Berlin to explore the problems. Hitler and Ribbentrop offered him grand if vague vistas of partitioning the British Empire, attempting to frustrate further Soviet moves westward, and to channel Russian expansionism toward the Persian Gulf and the

Indian Ocean where the Soviets would clash with the British. But Molotov stubbornly insisted on discussing German moves in the Balkans and where the USSR belonged in the Axis Triplice. The negotiations got nowhere.

On November 25, Stalin proposed to Hitler that the Triplice be broadened to include Russia and transformed into a Four-Power Pact. But there were a number of conditions that had to be fulfilled. The Germans were to pull their troops out of Finland, the Japanese were to surrender their concessions on northern Sakhalin, and Bulgaria and Turkey were to grant concessions and bases to the Soviets. Hitler made no reply; he had already decided on war.

A little less than a month later, on December 21, 1940, the German General Staff completed historic Directive Number 21, the plans for "Operation Barbarossa," and Hitler set the invasion deadline for May 15, 1941. "Barbarossa" called for a lightning five-month campaign which would simultaneously smash the Soviet state and crush the Red Armies. Panzer spearheads were to thrust deep into Russia, encircling and destroying Soviet combat formations and preventing them from trading "space for time" by retreat into the vast Russian hinterland.

The invasion was delayed five weeks because of Yugoslav, Greek, and British resistance to the German campaign in the Balkans. Those five weeks were to prove crucial. On Sunday morning, at 5:30 A.M., on June 22, 1941, 135 German, Finnish, and Romanian divisions raced forward on a 1500-mile front from the Baltic to the Black Sea. The Germans were divided into three great Army Groups. The Northern, based on East Prussia, was under the command of Wilhelm von Leeb and was to invest Leningrad and join with Finnish

German infantry was hard put to keep up with its galloping armor which smashed the Russian tanks in its path (below). Only the remains of burnt-out villages broke the monotony of the seemingly endless plains and forests. Three great German armies moved deeper into Russia: one headed for the Caucasus, a second for Moscow, and a third for Leningrad.

At Stalin's orders the Russians adopted a policy of "scorched earth." Every-

forces driving south under Marshal Mannerheim. The
Central Army Group was commanded by Fedor von
Bock, based on central Poland, and was to plunge
straight toward Moscow via Minsk and Smolensk. The
Southern Group was led by Karl von Rundstedt who was
to press into the Ukraine, the Donets Basin, and the
Caucasus. Here, the Soviets had their granary, major
sources of coal, iron ore, pig iron, manganese, and 85
per cent of Russia's oil. Facing them, the Russians
had disposed 186 divisions under Klementi Voroshilov
in the north, Semën Timoshenko in the center, and
Semën Budyenny in the south.

Churchill and Roosevelt had warned Stalin of the
impending onslaught, but the Russians were taken by
surprise because he had not believed them. A large
part of the Red Air Force was smashed on its airdromes
by the Luftwaffe, and the Nazi ground forces rolled
over bewildered Red Army formations. Instead of

thing was burned to deprive the Nazis of quarters during the winter ahead.

following the purged Marshal Tuchachevski's plan for meeting invasion with small forces, pulling back into Russia's vast depth, Stalin met the Germans with large armies at the border. This was exactly what Hitler and his generals wanted: speedy envelopment and annihilation of the largest part of Russia's armed forces as close to the forward areas as possible.

For 25 years Churchill had been an arch-opponent to Communism, but when queried about what he would do if the Nazis invaded the USSR, he replied: "I have only one purpose, the destruction of Hitler. . . . If Hitler invaded Hell I would make at least a favourable reference to the Devil in the House of Commons." With the onset of the invasion, Churchill immediately declared Britain's solidarity with the Soviet Union in resisting Nazi aggression.

Any man or state who fights on against Nazidom will have our aid. Any man or state who marches with

Hitler is our foe.... That is our policy and that is our declaration. It follows, therefore, that we shall give whatever help we can to Russia and the Russian people. We shall appeal to all our friends and allies in every part of the world to take the same course and pursue it, as we shall faithfully and steadfastly to the end....

Promise of American aid and support were immediately forthcoming, and Stalin told his people that they were not alone. He called on them for valor and daring in facing the enemy, and a policy of "scorched earth" if forced to retreat. Sabotage and wrecking was to destroy everything that might be of use to the enemy, and unrelenting guerrilla warfare was to be carried on in the Nazi rear.

The Nazi legions' initial successes were spectacular. Everywhere along the front they drove ahead from 200 to 400 miles in the first month. Von Bock was particularly successful on the central front where, after fighting two giant "battles of annihilation," at Minsk and Smolensk, he had not only captured unbelievable numbers of prisoners, but in eighteen days had thrust two-thirds of the way to Moscow. But even with these brilliant encirclements General von Bock had not been able to trap and destroy all of the Russian forces in the sector.

One of von Bock's generals, Gunther Blumentritt, described some of the early battles:

The infantry had a hard time keeping up. Marches of twenty-five miles in the course of a day were by no means exceptional, and that over the most atrocious roads. A vivid picture which remains of these weeks is the great clouds of yellow dust kicked up by the Russian columns attempting to retreat and by our infantry hastening in pursuit. The heat was tremendous, though interspersed with sudden showers which quickly turned the roads to mud before the sun reappeared and as quickly baked them into crumbling clay once again.

By 2 July the first battle was for all intents and purposes won. The haul was astounding. A hundred and fifty thousand prisoners taken, some twelve hundred tanks and six hundred guns captured or destroyed. First impressions revealed that the Russian was as tough a fighter as ever. His tanks, however, were not particularly formidable and his air force, so far as we could see, non-existent.

The conduct of the Russian troops, even in this first battle, was in striking contrast to the behaviour of the Poles and of the Western allies in defeat. Even when encircled, the Russians stood their ground and fought. The vast extent of the country, with its forests and swamps, helped them in this. There were not enough German troops available completely to seal off a huge encirclement such as that of Bialystok-Slonim. Our motorized forces fought on or near to the roads: in the great trackless spaces between them the Russians were able not infrequently to break out of our encirclements, whole columns moving by night through the forests that stretched away eastwards. They always attempted to break out to the east, so that the eastern side of each encirclement had to be held by our strongest troops, usually Panzer troops. Nevertheless, our encirclements were seldom entirely successful.

The German High Command wanted to concentrate on the central front and send von Bock's tanks crashing through to take Moscow, the capital and nerve center of resistance. They wanted to strike hard before the Red Army could recover and regroup. But Hitler disagreed. He was anxious to capture Leningrad and also to cut off Russia's oil supplies from the Caucasus. He

141

Though Hitler had gone into Russia with 175 divisions, by fall the casualty lists were beginning to alarm his generals. Many units were seriously understrength. Hitler, however, expected to triumph before winter.

The crew of a Russian anti-tank gun takes a near-miss during an attack. Russian equipment was rarely a match for the German at this stage of the war. The Nazis owned the air.

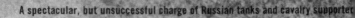
A spectacular, but unsuccessful charge of Russian tanks and cavalry supported

by planes. The West abandoned cavalry; Russia still used mounted units.

detached Panzer groups from von Bock's wings to help von Leeb invest Leningrad and to help von Rundstedt in the vast encirclement battles around Kiev. Von Bock's progress was halted for a critical two months.

In late September, after von Bock's columns had helped von Rundstedt capture more than 600,000 prisoners in a tremendous encirclement battle near Kiev, Hitler permitted von Bock to resume his offensive. In a violent attack, beginning October 6, von Bock drove forward 150 miles more in three weeks. Between Vyazma and Bryansk he captured another 600,000 prisoners, and then plunged toward Moscow. By mid-October he was attacking Moscow from three sides and the capital was almost surrounded. On October 17, the Soviet government, industry and non-essential civilians, were evacuated from Moscow and sent to Kuibyshev, behind the Ural Mountains. Only Stalin remained in the Kremlin to direct the battle for Moscow. Henry Cassidy, an American newsman, tells what the city was like at that time:

The people of Moscow were called upon to play a major part in the drama of life or death of their city. . . . Thousands of women, mobilized by their house committees and still wearing their city clothes, went by train, bus, and truck into the mud, slush and cold west of Moscow, there to dig tremendous trenches and anti-tank ditches, running like scars across the countryside. The fortifications extended back into the city itself, where steel, sandbag, and earthwork barricades were raised. The Palace of Soviets, a naked skeleton of steel girders, which was to have risen as the world's highest building, started to come down as raw material for defense. The Moscow Metro, most modern subway system in the world, was given over to movements of troops and supplies.

Part of the long lines of Russian prisoners which were marched back to Ger-

In all small shops which were not evacuated, work was turned entirely to war orders. One, which had been making pots and pans, started turning out hand-grenades. Another, which usually made cash registers and adding machines, began producing automatic rifles. . . .

When the mass evacuation began October 15, there were three days of stampede. People swarmed the railroad stations, seeking transportation, and when there was none, started on foot into the vast spaces

many. On two occasions, half a million men were captured during one battle.

of the east. Queues formed at food stores for the extra rations of bread, sausage, and cheese allotted to evacuées. There was a boom on the matrimonial market, as people married to go along with others whose offices or factories were being evacuated....

In November, rain bogged the Nazi Panzers down in a sea of mud and then the fierce Russian winter loosed its freezing snow and bitter cold early. German columns pressed forward slowly to within twenty miles of Moscow, and on December 2, advance infantry units penetrated the outskirts of the capital, so close that they could see the onion-shaped towers of the Kremlin. But the Germans had lost their desperate race against winter, and they had to retreat. General Blumentritt described their situation:

And now, when Moscow itself was almost in sight, the mood both of commanders and troops changed. With amazement and disappointment we discovered in late October and early November that the beaten Russians seemed quite unaware that as a military force they had almost ceased to exist. . . . Skillfully camouflaged strongpoints, wire entanglements and thick minefields now filled the forests which covered the western approach to Moscow.

One began to hear sarcastic references to the military leaders far away in Germany. The troops felt that it was high time our political leaders came and had a look at the front. Our soldiers were over-tired now, our units under strength. This was particularly so among the infantry, where many companies were reduced to a mere sixty or seventy men. The horses, too, had suffered grievously and the artillery had difficulty moving its guns. The number of serviceable tanks in the Panzer divisions was far below establishment. Since Hitler had believed that the campaign was over, he had ordered that industry at home cut down on its production of munitions. Only a trickle of replacements reached the fighting units. Winter was about to begin, but there was no sign of any winter clothing to be seen anywhere.

Hitler, who had anticipated a five-month blitzkrieg, had provided winter uniforms for only one man in five. Heinrich Haape, a medical officer who saw it, was moved:

On 13 November we awoke and shivered. Any icy blast from the north-east knifed across the snowy

As autumn came, the churned up Russian roads slowed the Panzers.

countryside. The sky was cloudless and dark blue, but the sun seemed to have lost its strength and instead of becoming warmer towards noon as on previous days, the thermometer kept falling and by sundown had reached minus twelve degrees Centigrade.

The soldiers who up to now had not regarded the light frosts too seriously began to take notice. One man who had been walking outside for only a short distance without his woolen Kopschutzer or 'head-saver' came into the sick bay. Both ears were white and frozen stiff. It was our first case of frost-bite. . . .

This minor case of frost-bite was a serious warning. The icy winds from Siberia — the breath of death — were

By the end of October, bad roads had become impossible roads. Hitler insisted on one more thrust toward Moscow, but by December it had broken down and the Wehrmacht was stuck in the mud to face Russia's winter.

Russian counterattacks during the winter of 1941-42 pushed the Germans back from advanced positions which Hitler insisted on holding against the advice of his generals. For the first time, the morale of the Nazis began to deteriorate.

blowing across the steppes; winds from where all life froze, from the Arctic ice-cap itself. Things would be serious if we could not house ourselves in prepared positions and buildings, and I stopped to think of the armies marching on Moscow across open country at this very moment. . . .

Those Arctic blasts that had taken us by surprise in our protected positions had scythed through our attacking troops. In a couple of days there were one hundred thousand casualties from frost-bite alone; one hundred thousand first-class, experienced soldiers fell out because the cold had surprised them. . . .

More and more reports were being sent to Corps and Army Headquarters recommending that the attack on Moscow by a summer-clad army be abandoned and that winter positions be prepared. Some of these reports were forwarded by Central Army Group to the Führer's Headquarters, but no reply or acknowledgement ever came. The order persisted: 'Attack!' And our soldiers attacked.

In the south, von Rundstedt too had gone from victory to victory. By November he had overrun the Ukraine and all of the Crimea except beleaguered Sevastopol, had sliced into the Donets Basin, and captured Rostov-on-Don, the gateway to the Caucasus. Like von Bock in the center and von Leeb in the north, von Rundstedt called for withdrawal to winter positions when the snows came. Hitler refused to abandon any of the territory conquered and insisted that he stand fast in Rostov against a Timoshenko counterattack. Rundstedt, believing this to be criminal stupidity, asked to be relieved. On December 3 he was succeeded by von Reichenau who abandoned Rostov and pulled his forces back to winter positions on the Mius, as von Rundstedt had asked to do.

On December 5, General Georgi Zhukov, who had replaced Timoshenko on the central front while Timoshenko relieved Budyenny in the south, launched a counterattack against von Bock's forces with fresh troops from the Far East and the new giant T-34 tanks. The Germans were driven back from 50 to a 100 miles from the capital and Moscow was saved.

As the Germans retreated along their entire battle line, Hitler furiously replaced general after general. Finally, Hitler himself assumed command.

The German troops fought not only General Zhukov but "General Winter." Heinrich Haape recorded their retreat before Moscow:

In this unearthly cold, in which the breath froze and icicles hung from nostrils and eyelashes all day long, where thinking became an effort, the German soldiers fought — no longer for an ideal or an ideology, no longer for the Fatherland. They fought blindly without asking questions, without wanting to know what lay ahead of them. Habit and discipline kept them going; that and the flicker of an instinct to stay alive. And when the soldier's mind had become numb, when his strength, his discipline and his will had been used up, he sank into the snow. If he was noticed, he was kicked and slapped into a vague awareness that his business in the world was not finished and he staggered to his feet and groped on. But if he lay where he had collapsed until it was too late, as if forgotten he was left dying at the side of the road and the wind blew over him and everything was levelled indistinguishably.

On December 8, Hitler finally had to admit defeat. He called a halt to military operations for the rest of the winter. In less than six months, his armies had penetrated 550 miles into the heart of European Russia and occupied more than 500,000 square miles of Soviet

A German infantryman lies frozen in the snow near the outskirts of Moscow.

territory. The Nazis admitted a cost of more than 740,000 of their troops killed, wounded, and missing, while the Russians listed their losses at almost three times that, at more than 2,100,000. The Germans, however, claimed more than 3,000,000 prisoners, not to speak of killed or wounded, and informed estimates make it seem likely that the Russians lost in the neighborhood of 6,000,000 men altogether.

Despite all that, Hitler had not achieved his fundamental goals. The Red Armies had not been decimated; Soviet industrial strength was sufficient to continue the war; and the Communist state had not collapsed. At first the invaders had been greeted as liberators in White Russia and the Ukraine and there were large-scale desertions to the Germans. But the Nazis killed, tortured and starved hundreds of thousands—deserters, prisoners, and populace alike. Germanic "superman" attempts to enslave the "inferior" Slavs swiftly alienated any who might have served the Germans. Ruthlessness and brutality ignited Russian resistance and they now fought against the invaders with the same cruelty and savagery as had been employed against them. Except for the Ukraine, there was no political collapse. Though there was political disaffection, Stalin's dictatorship held firm reins on the people; and the rapid restoration in July of the political commissars to prominence in the Red Army reasserted Communist Party control there. But the thousands of torn-up Party cards lying in Moscow streets, when the Nazis were at the gates, were only one obvious manifestation of hatred of the regime, and Stalin was shrewd enough to note it. Soviet propaganda immediately took advantage of the Russian's fierce love of his homeland, and a new note was struck: a great patriotic war in defense, not of Communism, but of Mother Russia.

Days of Infamy

The War in Asia

The outbreak of war in Europe provoked a choice for Japan's leaders. On one hand, as in World War I, they could profit from the war by peaceful commercial expansion without paying the terrible cost of conquest in blood and treasure. On the other hand, they could now more easily seize what they wanted by force. Trade and economic self-interest, however, meant disentangling themselves from the "China Incident," and this the military was dead set against. The fighting services felt that giving up what they had conquered in China by ten years of blood would be a confession that their program for Japan's welfare by conquest was bankrupt. Peaceful trade was not only humiliating for them, but would also surely loosen their hold on the government at home.

While Britain and France concentrated on the Nazi threat, the Japanese made the most of their opportunity in Asia. On February 10, 1939, they seized Hainan and on March 3 the Spratly Islands, both claimed by France. The two islands in the China Sea were strategically astride the sea lanes from Singapore to Hong Kong. In June, the Japanese increasingly brought pressure to bear on the International Settlements in Shanghai, Tientsin, and Kulangsu, and deliberately harassed British shipping. Japan's purpose was to destroy foreign commercial interests in China and cut off foreign aid to Chiang Kai-shek. Though Prime Minister Chamberlain, under heavy fire in Europe, was willing to accept Japan's "special status" in China, the United States was not. On July 6, in reprisal for Japanese intimidations and interference with American interests, Secretary of State Cordell Hull denounced the Commercial Treaty of 1911, to become effective six months

Japanese troops celebrate a victory in China (above). (Below) General Hideki Tojo at a press conference in October, 1941, when he was called on to form a new cabinet. The replacement of the moderate Konoye with Tojo made war certain.

later on January 26, 1940, when the treaty was to expire. In addition, in September, FDR embargoed deliveries of scrap steel and iron, loaned another $25,000,000 to Chiang, and advised American citizens in the Far East to return home.

The Nazi blitzkriegs against Poland, Norway, the Low Countries, and France gave Japan new openings. Once the war was on, the hard-pressed Allies were intent on keeping Japan from joining the Nazis and willing to make more concessions. On June 24, the Japanese forced the British to close the Burma Road to China for three months. At the same time, the fall of France permitted Japanese incursions into Indochina. In June, the Japanese forced France to close the Indochinese border, and in September, under combined German and Japanese pressures, Vichy conceded Japan air and military bases in French Indochina. The Japanese stepped up their infiltration of Siam (or Thailand), and simultaneously demanded economic concessions from the Dutch East Indies.

The brilliant Nazi military successes not only led to Japan's signing the Tri-Partite Pact that same month, on September 27, thus changing the 1936 Anti-Comintern Pact into a military alliance with the Axis, but also encouraged the Japanese militarists. They proceeded to tighten their hold on the reins of government, abolishing the political parties during that summer, and setting up a new, single, totalitarian party, the Imperial Rule Assistance Association.

The August 1939 Nazi-Soviet Pact had left the pro-Axis and anti-Communist Japanese military high and dry. Having once turned his own Drang nach Osten into a blitzkrieg against the West, Hitler encouraged Japan not to attack his new Soviet ally. But even after Nazi successes in 1940, Britain still stood uninvaded and

Japan moved cautiously. When Japanese Foreign Minister Yosuke Matsuoka visited Berlin in March 1941, Hitler deliberately did not tell him that the Wehrmacht would invade Russia in June. Nor did he object to Matsuoka's proposal for a neutrality pact between Japan and the USSR. On his way home, Matsuoka stopped in Moscow and there, on April 13, 1941, signed a five-year non-aggression pact with Stalin, who cordially assured him that they were both "Asiatics." Stalin was freed by the pact to concentrate on the threat of Hitler; Japan was freed to strike south against the British, Dutch, and Americans.

After the Germans attacked Russia, Hitler tried to persuade Japan to turn about again, and attack the Soviet Union. Although Matsuoka was for it, the Army vetoed it. The Japanese military was convinced it had nothing to gain by fighting Russia. If the Nazis defeated the Soviets, they could then take what they wanted in Siberia and Mongolia anyway.

What Japan needed was food, rubber, tin, nickel, chrome, iron, lumber, and that most basic of necessities for modern war, oil. All were to the south, in Indochina, Malaya, the Philippines, and the Dutch East Indies. Between July 1940 and spring 1941, America had cut its trade with Japan down to a trickle. Because it had formerly supplied the major part of Japan's high-octane gasoline, autos, planes, scrap iron and steel, copper, and other commodities, the American blockade made rapid action more imperative. Though Britain was in dire straits, having suffered defeat after defeat in Greece, Crete, and North Africa, and severe damage to its Mediterranean Fleet from Luftwaffe bombings, after three months were up, it had reopened the Burma Road to China. And though the Netherlands had fallen to Hitler, the Dutch, supported by America and Britain, had

In 1940, Japan had decided to join the Axis, and Saburo Kurusu, the ambass

prolonged the negotiations on oil concessions but given up nothing by June 1941. On July 2, an Imperial Conference decided to move south even at the risk of war with Britain and the U. S. Thus 50,000 troops were swiftly landed in Indochina and made it a Japanese protectorate.

Allied reaction was equally swift. On July 24, the United States froze all Japanese assets. Britain, the Dominions, and the Netherlands quickly did the same. Virtually all commercial and financial transactions between them and Japan ceased. The intensified blockade

dor in Berlin (above, left), signed a military pact with Germany and Italy.

was of critical importance to the Japanese. The Island Empire, under such expanding economic pressure, would have to deplete its raw materials stockpiles. If these continued to dwindle, Japan would soon be unable to fight. But before the Army decided to smash the ABCD (America-Britain-China-Dutch) blockade and take the natural resources it coveted by force, it gave Premier Fumimaro Konoye one more chance to see if some way out of the impasse could be negotiated.

Earlier, in February 1941, as Japan dipped increasingly into its raw material accumulations, Konoye had sent a new ambassador to the United States, Admiral Kichisaburo Nomura, to do the job. The month before, on January 27, American Ambassador to Japan Joseph C. Grew had sent a warning cable to Hull: A MEMBER OF THE EMBASSY WAS TOLD BY MY PERUVIAN COLLEAGUE THAT FROM MANY QUARTERS, INCLUDING A JAPANESE ONE, HE HAD HEARD THAT A SURPRISE MASS ATTACK ON PEARL HARBOR WAS PLANNED BY THE JAPANESE MILITARY FORCES, IN CASE OF "TROUBLE" BETWEEN JAPAN AND THE UNITED STATES; THAT THE ATTACK WOULD INVOLVE THE USE OF ALL JAPANESE MILITARY FORCES. MY COLLEAGUE SAID THAT HE WAS PROMPTED TO PASS THIS ON BECAUSE IT HAD COME TO HIM FROM MANY SOURCES, ALTHOUGH THE PLAN SEEMED FANTASTIC. It was soon to seem less fantastic.

What Japan wanted was recognition of its "New Order" in Asia. Nomura attempted to get the U. S. to accept several basic conditions, among them Japanese domination of China, unfreezing of Japanese assets, resumption of trade, and American help in getting vital raw materials for Japan. The U. S., however, would agree to restoration of trade only after Japan had evacuated its troops from all of China and Indochina, after Japan agreed to respect the territorial and political integrity of Chiang Kai-shek's government, after Japan agreed to equality of economic opportunity in China, and after Japan agreed to use only peaceful means to revise the Far Eastern status quo.

The two positions were irreconcilable. The Japanese Army refused to give up its spoils of war in China or its sense of Japan's unique role in Asia. America refused a Far Eastern Munich at China's expense, would not accept a settlement based on leaving Japan the fruits of its aggressions, and would not agree to a Japanese-dominated "New Order" in Asia. Konoye invited

Roosevelt to a meeting in Honolulu for further discussions, but FDR declined unless new proposals were forthcoming beforehand. As a result, the Konoye Cabinet fell on October 18, and arch-militarist General Hideki Tojo became Premier. On November 17 he sent a special envoy, Saburo Kurusu, in a final attempt to achieve U. S. acceptance of Japanese claims through diplomacy, but Kurusu brought no new undertakings. The talks in Washington continued, fruitlessly, but the Japanese had already put their war plans in motion.

Pearl Harbor

The Japanese hoped for a short, limited war to achieve their economic and political goals. They planned a raid to smash the American fleet at Pearl Harbor which, in a single surprise stroke, would give them naval superiority in the Pacific and so leave the road open for their conquest of Southeast Asia. Once they had taken their objectives, they planned to build around their conquests a defensive perimeter so strong

On December 7, 1941, Special Envoy Kurusu and Ambassador Nomura leave the State Department after seeing Cordell Hull. The sneak attack started only hours later.

Japanese sailors cheer as carrier planes take off to attack Pearl Harbor (above). (Below) a "Val" dive bomber goes in. The job was done with torpedo planes and bombers. But American carriers were not in port.

that it would be too expensive in human lives for the United States to break through it. They then imagined they could effect a negotiated peace leaving Japan free to consolidate and develop its Greater East Asia Co-Prosperity Sphere.

Planning had begun almost a year before, but final action was formulated in September and October, and on November 5 and 7 came Combined Fleet Top Secret Orders Number 1 and 2 for coordinated attacks on Pearl Harbor, Malaya, the Philippines and the Dutch East Indies. The attack on Pearl Harbor was to be made without a declaration of war so that if it failed the Emperor could repudiate it as the work of unauthorized hotheads.

On November 22, while Kurusu and Nomura, probably unwittingly, went ahead with their negotiations in Washington, a Japanese fleet surreptitiously assembled in Tankan Bay in the Kurile Islands. The 32-ship task force commanded by Vice-Admiral Chuichi Nagumo included 6 aircraft carriers, 2 battle ships, 2 heavy and 1 light, cruisers and a covering force of submarines, destroyers, and tankers. On November 26 they sailed, keeping far to the north of Hawaii, and under orders not to break radio silence. Six days later, on December 2, the man who had masterminded the operation, Admiral Isoroku Yamamoto, radioed Nagumo the code signal to attack Pearl Harbor—"Climb Mount Niitaka." Nagumo turned his fleet south and raced for Hawaii.

Although American Naval Intelligence had broken both the Japanese military and naval codes, and was deciphering a large number of Japanese messages, it knew nothing of Nagumo's striking force. Washington had been informed of ominous developments in the Gulf of Siam where Japanese convoys had been sighted heading for either Malaya or Siam. In a last-ditch effort

175

Blazing, the battleship Arizona lists to starboard just before going down.

to have them turn back, President Roosevelt addressed a personal message to Emperor Hirohito on December 6. But it was too late. The die was cast and Nagumo's carriers were bearing down on the Hawaiian Islands.

Through MAGIC, the name for secret decoding of Japanese messages, Washington had for some time been aware of Japan's unrelenting position. On November 27, 1941, Washington had warned Rear Admiral Husband E. Kimmel and Major General Walter C. Short at Pearl Harbor to be alert, but had apparently failed to communicate its own sense of urgency to the two commanders. Virtually no long-range aerial reconnaissance or naval patrol were scheduled for the areas around Oahu. Few anti-aircraft precautions had been taken, and ships and defense installations were not on the alert. The naval vessels in the harbor and the planes on the Oahu airfields were lined up neatly, like sitting ducks. Fortunately, the major Japanese targets, the American carriers, had left Pearl Harbor with their escorting cruisers for naval exercises at Wake and Midway Islands.

Sunday, December 7, 1941, was a calm, sunny morning in Honolulu. At 6 A.M., about 230 miles north of Oahu, 353 Japanese planes were taking off into the dawn from Admiral Nagumo's carriers. At 6:45 A.M., the American destroyer Ward sighted a Japanese midget submarine. It fired its guns at it, and dropped depth charges. Its commander immediately reported that they had done so but confusion about whether his radiogram meant that he had really seen the sub, or merely had an "underwater contact," prevented declaration of an alert. At 7:02 A.M., U. S. Army Privates Joseph L. Lockard and George Elliott, watching their radarscope at Opana, near Haleiwa, north of Pearl Harbor, picked up a large flight of airplanes approach-

(Above) Flaming ships on Battleship Row. Eight battleships were knocked out during the attack, though some returned to fight later in the war. Planes (below) died on the ground as the Japanese bombers attacked twice within two hours.

ing from the north. When they reported it to the officer in charge, Lieutenant Kermit Tyler, he told them to forget it. A dozen B-17 Flying Fortresses were due to arrive from the mainland that morning and Tyler was sure that their flight explained the radar blips.

Commanding the Japanese attack force was Mitsuo Fuchida, who flew in the lead plane of the first wave.

The weather was far from ideal. A 20-knot northeast wind was raising heavy seas. Flying at 3000 meters, we were above a dense cloud layer which extended down to within 1500 meters of the water. The brilliant morning sun had just burst into sight, setting the eastern horizon aglow.

One hour and forty minutes after leaving the carriers I knew that we should be nearing our goal. Small openings in the thick cloud cover afforded occasional

In addition to attacking warships in the harbor and grounded aircraft, the

glimpses of the ocean, as I strained my eyes for the first sight of land. Suddenly a long white line of breaking surf appeared directly beneath my plane. It was the northern shore of Oahu.

Veering right toward the west coast of the island, we could see that the sky over Pearl Harbor was clear. Presently the harbor itself became visible across the central Oahu plain, a film of morning mist hovering over it. I peered intently through my binoculars at the ships riding peacefully at anchor. One by one I counted them. Yes, the battleships were there all right, eight of them! But our last lingering hope of finding any carriers present was now gone. Not one was to be seen.

It was 0749 when I ordered my radioman to send the command, "Attack!" He immediately began tapping out the prearranged code signal: "TO, TO, TO . . ."

Japanese hit shore installations; but most of the damage was quickly repaired.

The repair crew at Hickam Field starts its work on a badly damaged bomber.

Leading the whole group, Lieutenant Commander Murata's torpedo bombers headed downward to launch their torpedoes, while Lieutenant Commander Itaya's bomber group climbed for altitude and was out of sight. My bombers, meanwhile, made a circuit toward Barbers Point to keep pace with the attack schedule. No enemy fighters were in the air, nor were there any gunflashes from the ground.

The effectiveness of our attack was now certain, and a message, 'Surprise attack successful!' was accordingly sent to Akagi at 0753. . . .

As the bombers completed their runs they headed north to return to the carriers. Pearl Harbor and the air bases had been pretty well wrecked by the fierce strafings and bombings. The imposing naval array of an hour before was gone. . . .

Two waves of Japanese planes struck at 7:55 and 8:40. By 10 o'clock it was all over. Dive bombers, torpedo planes, high-altitude bombers, and strafing fighters had left Pearl Harbor a blazing shambles. Of the 96 men-of-war anchored in the harbor, they sank or disabled 18—among them 8 battleships and 3 cruisers. Of 394 aircraft parked on the four airdromes, 108 were destroyed and 159 damaged. American casualties were 2343 dead, 960 missing, and 1172 wounded. The Japanese suffered only minor losses: 29 planes, 55 men, a submarine, and a few midget subs. With one boldly conceived and brilliantly executed stroke, the Japanese had put a large part of American naval and air power in the Far East out of commission.

But the attack had not been an unqualified success. The U. S. aircraft carriers, cruisers, submarines, and all but three destroyers escaped, so that within six months, American naval power in the Pacific, reinforced by units from the Atlantic Fleet, was able to slash Japanese fleets at Coral Sea and Midway. Also, the Japanese had failed to destroy Pearl Harbor's shore installations, its docks, fuel storage tanks, and ship-repair facilities, which would have forced the Pacific Fleet back to the West Coast of the United States. The next day, President Roosevelt told the Congress: **Yesterday, December 7, 1941 — a date which will live in infamy — the United States of America was suddenly and deliberately attacked by naval and air forces of the Empire of Japan.**

Congress promptly voted for war on the entire Axis.

Malaya and Singapore

The Japanese moved with blitzkrieg swiftness and efficiency. On the same day as Pearl Harbor, amphibious assault forces landed in Malaya and Thailand. From Singapore, Admiral Tom Phillips led a British naval squadron north to intercept the troop transports and landing craft. The new 35,000-ton battleship Prince of Wales, the 32,000-ton battlecruiser Repulse, and four destroyers sailed without air cover. Japanese submarines and reconnaissance aircraft discovered the flotilla and Japanese torpedo and dive bombers caught it and sent both the big ships to the bottom. Cecil Brown, on board the Repulse, describes the naval debacle:

11:15 — The guns of the Prince of Wales just let go. At the same instant I see the flame belching from the guns of the Wales, ours break into a chattering, ear-splitting roar. The nine Japanese aircraft are stretched out across the bright, blue, cloudless sky like star sapphires of a necklace.

I gape open-mouthed at those aircraft coming directly over us, flying so that they will pass from bow

to stern over the Repulse. The sky is filled with black puffs from our ack-ack. They seem a discordant profanation of that beautiful sky. But the formation of Japanese planes, coming over one behind the other, is undisturbed.

Now they are directly overhead. For the first time I see bombs coming down, materializing suddenly out of nothingness and streaming toward us like everenlarging tear-drops. There's a magnetic, hypnotic, limb-freezing fascination in that sight.

It never occurs to me to try and duck or run. Openmouthed and rooted, I watch the bombs getting larger and larger. Suddenly, ten yards from me, out in the water, a huge geyser springs out of the sea, and over the side, showering water over me and my camera.

I instinctively hunch over, sort of a semi-crouch, and at the same instant there is a dull thud. The whole ship shudders. . . .

11.51½ — Captain Tennant is sending a message to the Wales: 'Have you sustained any damage?'

The answer comes back: 'We are out of control. Steering gear is gone.'

12.20 — The communication pipes again, 'Stand by for barrage!' and hell breaks loose again. A plane is diving straight for the middle of the ship off the port side, five hundred yards away, and tracers are rushing to meet it, but it comes on. Now it seems suspended in the air one hundred above the water, and the torpedo drops.

It is streaking for us. There is a deadly fascination in watching it. The watcher shouts, 'Stand by for torpedo!' The torpedo strikes the ship about twenty yards astern of my position. It feels as though the ship has crashed into dock. I am thrown four feet across the deck but I keep my feet. Almost immediately, it

189

Japanese air power reigned supreme. The British battleship Prince of Wa

seems, the ship lists.

The command roars out of the loudspeaker: 'Blow up your life belts!'...

The Repulse is going down.

The torpedo-smashed Prince of Wales, still a half to three-quarters of a mile ahead, is low in the water, half shrouded in smoke, a destroyer by her side.

Japanese bombers are still winging around like vul-

...d the cruiser Repulse (above) were sent to the bottom by torpedo planes.

tures, still attacking the Wales. A few of those shot down are bright splotches of burning orange on the blue South China Sea.

Men are tossing overboard rafts, life-belts, benches, pieces of wood, anything that will float. . . .

Men are jumping into the sea from the four or five defense control towers that segment the main mast like a series of ledges. One man misses his distance,

Singapore victims of the swift Japanese drive in South Asia.

Japanese infantry (above) and armor (below) pushed into Burma against mixed British-American forces commanded by General Sir Harold Alexander, later to become famous in Italy, and the American "Vinegar Joe" Stilwell. Stilwell's forces were principally Chinese and Burmese. The Japanese pushed the Allies clean out of Burma and back into India.

dives, hits the side of the Repulse, breaks every bone in his body and crumples into the sea like a sack of wet cement. . . .

Fifty feet from the ship, hardly swimming at all now, I see the bow of the Repulse swing straight into the air like a church steeple. Its red under plates stand out as stark and as gruesome as the blood on the faces of the men around me. Then the tug and draw of the suction of 32,000 tons of steel sliding to the bottom hits me. Something powerful, almost irresistible snaps at my feet. It feels as though someone were trying to pull my legs out by the hip sockets. But I am more fortunate than some others. They are closer to the ship. They are sucked back.

General Tomoyuki Yamashita's troops, whose landing the Wales and Repulse had been sent to frustrate, drove down both sides of the Malay Peninsula toward Singapore. Outfitted for and skilled in jungle warfare, the Japanese combined infiltration, flanking movements, and amphibious small-boat landings in the rear of the bewildered British, Australian, and Malay troops, and drove them back. By the end of January, the Japanese had conquered all Malaya and were besieging the Singapore fortress. On February 15 General Arthur Percival surrendered almost 60,000 troops, and Singapore.

General Harold Alexander, in command of British and Indian troops, and American General Joseph W. Stilwell, since March 1942 Chiang Kai-shek's chief of staff, and commanding Chinese troops in Burma, both managed to extricate most of their men from Burma and, after losing all their heavy equipment, marching the long, bitter way into Assam and Bengal. "Vinegar Joe" Stilwell, no diplomat, summed up the campaign succinctly: I claim we got a hell of a beating. We got run out of Burma, and it is humiliating as hell.

195

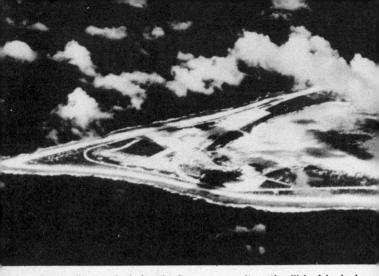

Tracers fill the air during the Japanese assault on tiny Wake Island wh

In December the Japanese had already captured their first footholds in the Indies in North Borneo and Sarawak. The major thrust came the next month, on the main island of Java. On January 23–25, American destroyers inflicted some minor losses on a Japanese convoy making for Java through the narrow Makassar Strait between that island and Celebes, but Japanese bombers sank the American airplane-tender Langley carrying fighter-plane reinforcements to Java. At the end of February, the critical battle for the Indies was fought in the Java Sea. In a three-day engagement, the Japanese Navy shattered a mixed squadron of Dutch, British, Australian, and American warships under Dutch Admiral Doorman, sinking five cruisers, six destroyers and a sloop with only the loss of one Japanese destroyer. Now, nothing stood in the path of the Japanese juggernaut, and on March 8, the government of the Netherlands East Indies surrendered.

400 Marines held out for sixteen days before finally being overpowered.

Between January and April the Japanese pushed their perimeter farther east by seizing the Admiralty and Gilbert Island chains, and by establishing themselves on the north shore of New Guinea. In February, Japanese bombers had hit the north Australian naval base at Port Darwin from their newly acquired airfields in Timor. By May, they were in closer bombing range of Australia from bases in New Guinea.

The smaller Allied outposts also caved in under the Japanese assault. After a 17-day siege beginning December 8, British Hong Kong surrendered on Christmas Day 1941 after the Japanese had overrun the city's water supplies. Unfortified Guam was taken five days after Pearl Harbor, on December 13, but on Wake Island, a detachment of less than 400 Marines held out for 16 days against an invasion force a hundred times its size. Battered from the air, the Marines threw back two landing attempts and sank two Japanese destroyers before being overpowered by swarms of Japanese. When the enemy was finally ashore, Major James P. Devereux, Marine commandant of the island, radioed: URGENT! ENEMY ON ISLAND. THE ISSUE IS IN DOUBT. On December 23, Wake surrendered. Of the three American island bases between Hawaii and the Philippines only Midway was left.

The Philippines

To protect Japan's invasions of Malaya and the Indies against interference from the U. S. Far Eastern Air Force and Asiatic Fleet, as well as because of the archipelago's strategic position, the Philippines were a major Japanese objective. Ten hours after Pearl Harbor, Japanese planes destroyed most of the American air force in the islands on the ground. This was due, in part, to a faulty warning system and, in part, to General Douglas MacArthur's refusal to send his B-17

American troops — wearing the old-fashioned. World War I tin hat — crouch in a

Flying Fortresses—the Far Eastern Air Force's Sunday punch—to bomb Japanese invasion bases on Hainan and Formosa until Congress had formally declared war.

Between December 8 and the end of the year, the Japanese virtually wiped out the American air force, based mainly at Clark and Nichols Fields in Luzon, and smashed the great naval base at Cavite, thereby forcing Admiral Thomas Hart to withdraw his small Asiatic Fleet to the Netherlands East Indies where it was eventually sent to the bottom in the Battle of the Java Sea. Though everything the Americans had left in the area, from lumbering PBY flying boats to B-17s, from submarines to PT-boats, was thrown into the breach, they were helpless to stop the Japanese landings, and were soon destroyed in action, crippled, or withdrawn.

With control of sea and air, the Japanese on Luzon were able to push swiftly out of their beachheads north and south of Manila and by the first of the new year had fought their way into the capital. American and

slit trench on Bataan during their four-month fight against heavy odds.

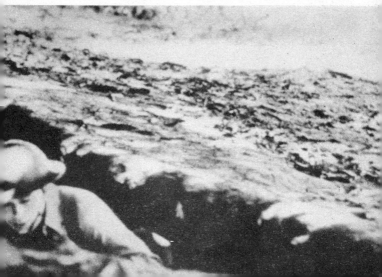

Weary defenders in one of the tunnels on rocky Corregidor island.

This fort near Manila held out until May against the enemy attacks.

Corregidor's big guns (above) were not able to stand up indefinitely against the pounding of Japanese artillery and bombers. One by one, they were put out of action (below) and the food inside the fortress dwindled to nothing.

Filipino forces, fighting desperate rearguard actions against overpowering numbers, pulled back to the rocky, jungle-covered Bataan Peninsula.

On Bataan and Corregidor, the island fortress at the tip of Bataan which secured the peninsula against seaborne invasion, Americans and Filipinos stood fast against the Japanese. But casualties, dwindling supplies, sickness, and American inability to reinforce or supply the garrison, gradually took its toll of the defenders. Somewhat bitterly they sang:

"We're the battling Bastards of Bataan;
No mama, no papa, no Uncle Sam;
No aunts, no uncles, no cousins, no nieces;
No pills, no planes, no artillery pieces
. . . And nobody gives a damn!"

On April 9, Bataan and its 40,000 battered defenders surrendered. Corregidor, "The Rock," under General Jonathan Wainwright, held out for another month, until May 6, 1942, when its 10,000 men finally capitulated.

On February 22, when the Philippine situation was obviously beyond repair, President Roosevelt ordered MacArthur evacuated to Australia. MacArthur left Wainwright in command and in a daring escape made his way to the land down under. There he declared:

The President of the United States ordered me to break through the Japanese lines and proceed from Corregidor to Australia for the purpose, as I understand it, of organizing the American offensive against Japan, a primary purpose of which is the relief of the Philippines. I came through and I shall return.

In combat, the Japanese were wily and savage, and ignored the rules of the Geneva Convention, which Japan had never signed. Where they conquered, atrocities were the order of the day. Rape, looting, killing, and merciless cruelty to prisoners not only shocked

203

Soldiers of Corregidor as the Japanese marched them into captivity.

General Douglas MacArthur as he arrived in Australia. President Roosevelt had ordered him to escape from the Philippines while there was time. Said MacArthur, "I shall return."

the white man but enraged him. The defeat the white man had suffered at Asiatic hands seriously undermined his prestige in Asia. Unfortunately, nowhere in Asia had the Allies given the native populations any real stakes in resisting the Japanese tide. In Malaya, Burma, Siam, and the Dutch East Indies native populations collaborated with the Japanese invaders. In India, Mahatma Gandhi and Congress Party leaders were imprisoned because, though the British promised them postwar independence, they called for passive resistance and refused to join in fighting the Japanese. Only in the Philippines, already guaranteed its independence in 1946 by the U. S., did native troops fight valiantly at the side of their American allies.

In five months the Japanese had conquered the great empire they had coveted for decades. With it they took almost 400,000,000 people and almost all the strategic materials they needed—oil, rubber, tin, tungsten, chrome, manganese and rice—except iron. The Japanese Imperial Navy now controlled most of the Pacific betwen Midway Island and the coast of China, and between the Aleutians and Australia, and a large part of the Indian Ocean as well. And the Japanese Imperial Army now held that formidable defense perimeter which they were sure was impervious to Allied counterattack.

All these objectives had been taken with 400,000 troops, only 20 per cent of Japanese land forces, and at a price of only 15,000 killed and wounded.

"Thirty Seconds over Tokyo"

Japan had underestimated American fighting spirit. Though Pearl Harbor had left the American Fleet greatly weakened, the Navy struck back within two months. On February 1, an American task force blasted the Marshall and Gilbert Islands. On February 24, American planes pounded Wake Island and on March 4, raided Marcus Island, less than 1000 miles from Tokyo. On March 10, carrier planes bombed the Japanese bases at Lae and Salamaua in New Guinea, and sank a converted light cruiser, a minesweeper and a freighter. But the Americans had a bigger surprise in store for the enemy; on April 18 came the first blow at Japan itself.

In a daring maneuver which had been planned as early as January, a task force with two carriers, the Enterprise and Hornet, moved to less than 700 miles from Tokyo to launch specially-equipped B-25 land-based bombers to strike at Japan. -There, spotted by Japanese patrol boats, and thinking they were discovered, the carriers sent their 16 Mitchell bombers aloft and turned back. Commanded by Colonel James Doolittle, the bombers headed for Tokyo, Nagoya, Osaka and Kobe.

Captain Ted Lawson, flying one of the planes, described his "thirty seconds over Tokyo":

... We came up over a hill, dusting the top of another temple, and there before us, as smooth as glass, lay Tokyo Bay. . . .

We were about two minutes out over the bay when we all of us seemed to look to the right at the same time, and there sat the biggest, fattest-looking aircraft carrier we had ever seen. It was a couple of miles away, anchored, and there did not seem to be a man in sight. It was an awful temptation not to change course and drop one on it. But we had been so drilled in what to do with our four bombs, and Tokyo was now so close that I decided to go on.

There were no enemy planes in sight. . . .

It took about five minutes to get across our arm of the bay, and, while still over the water, I could see the barrage balloons strung between Tokyo and Yoko-hama, across the river from Tokyo. . . .

I was almost on the first of our objectives before I saw it. I gave the engines full throttle as Davenport adjusted the prop pitch to get a better grip on the air. We climbed as quickly as possible to fifteen hundred feet, in the manner which we had practiced for a month and had discussed for three additional weeks.

There was just time to get up there, level off, attend to the routine of opening the bomb bay, make a short run and let fly with the first bomb. The red light blinked on my instrument board, and I knew the first 500-pounder had gone.

Our speed was picking up. The red light blinked again, and I knew Clever had let the second bomb go. Just as the light blinked, a black cloud appeared about a hundred yards or so in front of us and rushed past at great speed. Two more appeared ahead of us, on about the line of our wing-tips, and they too swept past. They had our altitude perfectly, but they were leading us too much.

The third red light flickered, and since we were now over a flimsy area in the southern part of the city, the fourth light blinked. That was the incendiary, which I knew would separate as soon as it hit the wind and that dozens of small fire bombs would molt from it.

The moment the fourth red light showed I put the nose of the Ruptured Duck into a deep dive.... Now, as I dived, I looked back and out: I got a quick indelible vision of one of our 500-pounders as it hit our steel-smelter target. The plant seemed to puff out its walls and then subside and dissolve in a black-and-red cloud....

I flattened out over a long row of low buildings and homes and got the hell out of there....

Our actual bombing operation, from the time the first one went until the dive, consumed not more than thirty seconds.

Those brief thirty seconds were momentous. They not only heartened Americans, but disconcerted the Japanese. Though Doolittle's bombers did only minor damage to the Japanese target cities, the raid probably

General (then Lieutenant Colonel) James Doolittle helps prepare one of the 500-pound bombs destined for Tokyo.

An Air Force B-25 Mitchell medium bomber as it roars down the deck of the carrier USS Hornet on its way to Tokyo. Sixteen B-25's did the job, operating from the Hornet and the Enterprise. The material damage they inflicted was small, but a blow against the homeland itself, previously considered invulnerable, gave Japan considerable pause.

encouraged Japanese leaders to expand their perimeter to protect the Japanese home islands from air attack, and certainly served to pin down badly needed Japanese fighter strength around Tokyo. President Roosevelt cryptically announced that the B-25s had come from Shangri-La, the fictitious utopian land of novelist James Hilton's book Lost Horizon, but the Japanese at first assumed that the planes actually came from Midway. They began to plan to seize Midway Island and then perhaps to invade Hawaii, for which Midway stood guard. Realizing their vulnerability, they moved to improve their defenses, but Doolittle's thirty seconds was to remain an ever-present source of concern as well as an omen of what was to come.

A B-25 bomber on its way to a momentous "thirty seconds over Tokyo."

credits

THE PHOTOGRAPHS

6-7 BIS
8-9 Wide World
10-11 Pix
14-15 BIS
16-17 New York Times
20-21 IWM
22-23 BIS
24-25 IWM
26-27 Wide World
28-29 BIS
30-31 Wide World
36-37 BIS
38-39 Wide World
40-41 BIS/Movietone News
42-43 IWM
44-45 IWM/Wide World
46-47 IWM
48-49 IWM
50-51 BIS/Wide World
52-53 UPI
54-55 IWM/Wide World
56-57 IWM
58-59 BIS
60-61 IWM
62-63 IWM
64-65 BIS
66-67 Robert Capa, Magnum
68-69 Wide World
72-73 European/Wide World
74-75 European
76-77 Wide World/UPI
78-79 Wide World
80-81 Wide World

82-83 Wide World/ Department of Defense
86-87 Wide World
88-89 Wide World
90-91 Wide World
92-93 Wide World
94-95 European
96-97 Wide World/OWI
100-101 European
102-103 European
104-105 Wide World
108-109 IWM/Wide World
112-113 Wide World
114-115 IWM
116-117 IWM
118-119 IWM
120-121 IWM
122-123 IWM
124-125 European
126-127 Wide World
128-129 Dever, Black Star
130-131 Ullstein
132-133 Ullstein
136-137 European/ Ullstein
138-139 Ullstein
142-143 European
144-145 Sovfoto
146-147 Sovfoto
148-149 Ullstein
150-151 Ullstein
152-153 Dever, Black Star
154-155 Ullstein/ European
156-157 Wide World
158-159 Sovfoto

162-163 Sovfoto
164-165 Combine
166-167 Combine/Wide World
170-171 Wide World
172-173 Wide World
174-175 Department of Defense/ Wide World
176-177 Department of Defense
178-179 Department of Defense
180-181 Wide World
182-183 Wide World
184-185 Department of Defense
186-187 Wide World
190-191 BIS
192-193 Combine
194-195 Department of Defense/ European
196-197 Department of Defense
198-199 Wide World
200-201 Department of Defense
202-203 Department of Defense
204-205 Wide World
206-207 Wide World
210-211 Wide World/ Department of Defense
212-213 Department of Defense

THE WORDS

16-20
Michie, Allan A. and Walter Graebner; from Their Finest Hour. © 1941 by TIME, Inc. Reprinted by permission of Harcourt, Brace & World, Inc. and George Allen & Unwin Ltd.

31-33
Leske, Gottfried; from I was a Nazi Flier. © 1941 by The Dial Press, Inc. Reprinted by permission of the publisher and author.

61-68
Moorehead, Alan; from African Trilogy. Hamish Hamilton Ltd., 1945. Reprinted by permission of Laurence Pollinger Ltd.

96-99
St. John, Robert; from From the Land of the Silent People. Doubleday & Co., © 1942 by Robert St. John.

103-110
Stephanides, Theodore; from Climax in Crete. Faber & Faber Ltd., London, 1946. Reprinted by permission of the publisher.

119
Wilmot, Chester; from Tobruk. Angus & Robertson Ltd., 1944. Reprinted by permission of the publisher.

120
Lambert, Eric; from The Twenty Thousand Thieves. Frederick Muller Ltd., London, 1952. Reprinted by permission of the publisher.

140-141
Blumentritt, Gunther (editors: Seymour Freidin and William Richardson); from The Fatal Decision. William Morrow & Co., Inc., © 1956 by William Sloane Associates, Inc. and Michael Joseph, Ltd. Reprinted with the permission of the publishers.

149-151
Cassidy, Henry C.; from Moscow Dateline. Houghton Mifflin Co., © 1943 by Henry Cassidy. Reprinted by permission of the author.

152
Blumentritt, Gunther (editors: Seymour Freidin and William Richardson); from The Fatal Decision. William Morrow & Co., Inc., © 1956 by William Sloane Associates, Inc. and Michael Joseph, Ltd. Reprinted with the permission of the publishers.

152-161
Haape, Heinrich and Dennis Henshaw; from Moscow Tram Stop. Collins Publishers, London; 4th November 1957; © 1962.

180-187
Fuchida, Mitsuo and Masatake Okumija (editors: Clarke Kawakami and Roger Pineau); from Midway: The Battle that Doomed Japan. © 1955 by U. S. Naval Institute, Annapolis, Md.

188-195
Brown, Cecil; from Suez to Singapore. © 1942 by Random House, Inc. Reprinted by permission of the publisher.

208-209
Lawson, Ted; from Thirty Seconds Over Tokyo. © 1943 by Random House, Inc. Reprinted by permission of the publisher.

The world at your fingertips

Leading historians, sociologists, political scientists, economists, and anthropologists offer personal and political analyses of the world's developing lands.

WE DELIVER!
And So Do These Bestsellers.

Bantam Book Catalog

Here's your up-to-the-minute listing of every book currently available from Bantam.

This easy-to-use catalog is divided into categories and contains over 1400 titles by your favorite authors.

So don't delay—take advantage of this special opportunity to increase your reading pleasure.

Just send us your name and address and 25¢ (to help defray postage and handling costs).